Abington Public Library
Abington, MA 02351

Real-World STEM:
Global Access to
Clean Water

Stuart A. Kallen

ReferencePoint
Press®

San Diego, CA

© 2018 ReferencePoint Press, Inc.
Printed in the United States

For more information, contact:
ReferencePoint Press, Inc.
PO Box 27779
San Diego, CA 92198
www.ReferencePointPress.com

ALL RIGHTS RESERVED.
No part of this work covered by the copyright hereon may be reproduced or used in any form or by any means—graphic, electronic, or mechanical, including photocopying, recording, taping, web distribution, or information storage retrieval systems—without the written permission of the publisher.

LIBRARY OF CONGRESS CATALOGING-IN-PUBLICATION DATA

Name: Kallen, Stuart A., 1955– author.
Title: Global Access to Clean Water/by Stuart A. Kallen.
Description: San Diego, CA: ReferencePoint Press, Inc., 2018. | Series:
   Real-World STEM series | Series: How clean water is provided—Pollution,
   waste, and drought —Transforming seawater to freshwater—Recycling
   wastewater—Transporting water | Includes bibliographical references and
   index. | Audience: 9 to 12.
Identifiers: LCCN 2016055245 (print) | LCCN 2017014801 (ebook) | ISBN
   9781682822449 (eBook) | ISBN 9781682822432 (hardback)
Subjects: LCSH: Water—Purification—Juvenile literature. |
   Water-supply—Juvenile literature.
Classification: LCC TD430 (ebook) | LCC TD430 .K355 2018 (print) | DDC
   628.1--dc23
LC record available at https://lccn.loc.gov/2016055245

CONTENTS

Great Engineering Achievements

1 ## Electrification
Vast networks of electricity provide power for the developed world.

2 ## Automobile
Revolutionary manufacturing practices made cars more reliable and affordable, and the automobile became the world's major mode of transportation.

3 ## Airplane
Flying made the world accessible, spurring globalization on a grand scale.

Water Supply and Distribution
Engineered systems prevent the spread of disease, increasing life expectancy.

4 **5** ## Electronics
First with vacuum tubes and later with transistors, electronic circuits underlie nearly all modern technologies.

7 **6** ## Radio and Television
These two devices dramatically changed the way the world receives information and entertainment.

Agricultural Mechanization
Numerous agricultural innovations led to a vastly larger, safer, and less costly food supply.

8 ## Computers
Computers are now at the heart of countless operations and systems that impact people's lives.

9 ## Telephone
The telephone changed the way the world communicates personally and in business.

10 ## Air Conditioning and Refrigeration
Beyond providing convenience, these innovations extend the shelf life of food and medicines, protect electronics, and play an important role in health care delivery.

Highways

Forty-four thousand miles of US highways enable personal travel and the wide distribution of goods.

11

12

Spacecraft

Going to outer space vastly expanded humanity's horizons and resulted in the development of more than sixty thousand new products on Earth.

Internet

The Internet provides a global information and communications system of unparalleled access.

13

Imaging

Numerous imaging tools and technologies have revolutionized medical diagnostics.

Household Appliances

These devices have eliminated many strenuous and laborious tasks.

15 **14**

Health Technologies

16

From artificial implants to the mass production of antibiotics, these technologies have led to vast health improvements.

Laser and Fiber Optics

Their applications are wide and varied, including almost simultaneous worldwide communications, noninvasive surgery, and point-of-sale scanners.

18 **17**

Petroleum and Petrochemical Technologies

These technologies provided the fuel that energized the twentieth century.

19

Nuclear Technologies

From splitting the atom came a new source of electric power.

20

High-Performance Materials

They are lighter, stronger, and more adaptable than ever before.

Source: Wm. A. Wulf, "Great Achievements and Grand Challenges," National Academy of Engineering, The Bridge, vol. 30, no. 3–4, Fall/Winter 2000. www.nae.edu/File.aspx?id=7327.

INTRODUCTION

Clean Water in a Dirty World

"All of the lakes [in Africa] are polluted and overdrawn, and the groundwater supplies and rivers are disappearing. Whole towns have no water whatsoever, and it is not uncommon for women to walk six hours a day to find water for their families."

—Maude Baow, global water expert

Quoted in Irene Salina, ed., *Written in Water.* Washington, DC: National Geographic Society, 2010.

In 2012 the National Aeronautics and Space Administration (NASA) released a photo titled *Blue Marble*—a picture of Earth taken 435 miles (700 km) above the planet. In the image, Earth and its deep blue oceans resemble a toy marble hanging in space. *Blue Marble* reminds people that most of Earth's surface is covered with water. And it quickly became one of the most widely viewed images on the Internet. As NASA scientist Robert Kandel comments, "Some would have us call our planet not 'Earth' but 'Ocean' in honor of the liquid vastness that covers over two-thirds of the globe."[1]

Water might cover a large percentage of the planet, but 98 percent of the liquid vastness is seawater, which is 3.5 percent salt. Saltwater is undrinkable—when ingested it causes massive dehydration and death. Seawater will also kill farm crops and livestock, making it useless for agricultural purposes. The survival of most plants and land animals is dependent on water without salt, or freshwater. But only 2 percent of the water on Earth is freshwater—and most of that is locked up in glaciers and ice caps. The freshwater available for human use—water found in lakes, rivers, streams, and underground deposits called aquifers—makes up less than 0.5 percent of all the water on the planet. To put this figure in perspective, if all the water on Earth could fit in a 1-gallon (3.8 L) bucket, only 1 tablespoon (15 mL) would be freshwater.

However, as journalist Steven Solomon explains, this water allows life to flourish: "Although the remarkably constant total volume of accessible, self-renewing freshwater is [extremely] tiny as a virtual few droplets of the planet's total water, it has sufficed to provide all of the water needed to support mankind throughout the entirety of human history—until today."[2]

Growing Demand, Shrinking Supply ■

Earth's population is predicted to soar past 8 billion by 2025, which means the demand for freshwater will grow every year. According to the United Nations (UN), China, India, and some African nations will need 50 percent more freshwater in the coming decades for human, agricultural, and industrial purposes. Developed countries, including the United States, are expected to increase water use by 18 percent.

WORDS IN CONTEXT

aquifer

sponge-like gravel and sand-filled underground reservoirs that contain naturally occurring freshwater

Population growth and water needs are already coming into conflict in China. The nation is home to 20 percent of the world's population but holds only 7 percent of the planet's freshwater. Put another way, China has as much water as Canada but around forty times more people. According to Jiao Yong, China's vice minister of water resources, at least four hundred cities in China are considered to be water scarce. Most of the half billion people living in those cities lack adequate clean water for drinking, cooking, and personal hygiene.

Even as global demand for freshwater grows, many of the sources of this water (rivers, streams, and lakes) are being used as dumps for industrial waste and human sewage. Water found aboveground in rivers, streams, and lakes is called surface water. In manufacturing nations from the United States to China, surface water is often tainted by toxic chemicals used to manufacture paints, pesticides, petroleum, plastics, and other products. In developing nations, such as India, Afghanistan, and countries in Africa, millions of people use rivers, lakes, and streams as toilets, polluting these waterways with raw sewage. The waste spreads harmful bacteria and parasites that cause diarrhea, dysentery,

Blue Marble, *the NASA photograph of Earth taken from hundreds of miles above the planet, clearly shows how much of the planet is covered by water. Unfortunately, 98 percent of that water is salty—rendering it undrinkable for humans and other animals and unusable for agriculture.*

cholera, and other severe ailments. Infants and young children are most affected by water polluted with human waste. According to the UN, every twenty-one seconds a child in a poor nation dies from drinking filthy water.

Can Engineers Fix These Problems? ■

Providing clean water to a thirsty world remains one of the ultimate engineering challenges of the twenty-first century. Many of the efforts focus on desalination: turning seawater into freshwater through processes that remove salt. But most desalination methods are energy intensive, meaning they require a lot of electricity to filter the salt out of the water. This makes desalination very expensive. Additionally, most desalination facilities rely on electricity produced by power plants that use fossil fuels: natural gas, coal, or oil. Scientists say that the burning of fossil fuels, considered to be a primary cause of climate change, may be reducing the world's freshwater supplies. Long-term droughts, which many scientists attribute to climate change, are drying up surface water sources across the globe.

WORDS IN CONTEXT

aqueduct

an artificial channel for conveying water, often consisting of a bridge supported by tall columns

Beyond desalination, engineers are looking to recycle wastewater. They are building technologically sophisticated treatment plants that turn treated sewage into sparkling-clean drinking water. Although many people are not yet sold on what is derisively referred to as the toilet-to-tap process, treating wastewater is the cheapest, most efficient way to provide the population with freshwater. The process, known as direct potable reuse, can also remove industrial pollutants often found in drinking water.

A new generation of pipelines, aqueducts, and pumping stations is also under consideration. In China, Africa, and the United States, massive engineering projects are being planned to move water from rainy areas to dry regions where it is needed the most.

The Basis of Life ■

Water is the basis of all life on Earth. The average person can only live three days without drinking water. But water is more than a basic human need. It has numerous uses in modern life. Today massive amounts of water are used to grow food, generate electricity, and produce cars, smartphones, and thousands of other products. Without freshwater, Earth would still look like a blue marble from space. But a closer examination would show people, plants, and animals struggling for survival. As dozens of clean water projects move forward across the globe, engineers are working against time to provide the freshwater supplies critical to daily life and all human endeavors.

CHAPTER 1

CURRENT STATUS: How Clean Water Is Provided

"For many of us, clean water is so plentiful and readily available that we rarely, if ever, pause to consider what life would be like without it."

—Marcus Samuelsson, restaurateur

Marcus Samuelsson, "Eat Out, Drink Up, and Save Lives," *Huffington Post*, May 25, 2011. www.huffingtonpost.com.

New York City is known for its arched bridges, thundering subways, and soaring skyscrapers. But one of the most essential pieces of engineering genius in New York is largely invisible to the city's photo-snapping tourists and 9.4 million residents. Every day the New York City water supply system provides 1.3 billion gallons (4.9 billion L) of drinking water to homes, apartments, offices, factories, public buildings, parks, and even urban farms.

Most of New York City's water comes from the Delaware River and other rivers that flow through the Catskill Mountains, around 125 miles (201 km) northeast of the city. The rivers feed a system of twenty-one reservoirs that connect to an extensive network of aqueducts, tunnels, and water mains (large pipes) that serve neighborhoods and individual buildings. If all of the city's aqueducts, tunnels, and pipes were laid end to end, they would stretch 6,500 miles (10,461 km). Water historian Gerard Koeppel calls the New York City system "the gold standard of urban water supplies."[3]

Most of the New York municipal water supply system was constructed during the twentieth century, and some parts are considered wonders of the industrial world. For example, the 163-mile-long (262 km) Catskill Aqueduct crosses under the Hudson River at a depth of 1,000 feet (305 m). The aqueduct was constructed between 1907 and 1916 with the era's most sophisticated rock drills and explosives. In 1909 the aqueduct was hailed as one of humanity's greatest engineering feats by Alfred Douglas Finn, a New York City water department engineer. In the national magazine *Century,* Finn compared the project to the construction of the Panama Canal, a shipping channel that connects the Atlantic and Pacific Oceans in Panama. Finn also pointed out the importance of the Catskill Aqueduct at a time when waterborne diseases killed millions throughout the world: "The need of the water is much greater than is realized by a majority of the citizens or by the guardians of their interests. Nothing can so quickly and completely disorganize the complex activities of a modern community as a shortage of suitable water; no single agency can so rapidly spread disease and death as a polluted water-supply."[4]

Taken for Granted

More than a century later, few New Yorkers ever think about the benefits of the Catskill Aqueduct or any of the other pieces of the New York City water system that functions efficiently far beneath the city streets. This lack of awareness prompts Jim Roberts, head of the city's Department of Environmental Protection, to state that

Few of those who live in or visit New York City (pictured) ever think about the municipal water supply system that includes a network of reservoirs, aqueducts, tunnels, and water pipes. This system provides freshwater to millions of people every day.

"so many New Yorkers take the amazing system that we have for granted. It is to a large extent out of sight and out of mind."[5]

New Yorkers are not the only Americans who take freshwater for granted. The United States is home to more than 152,000 municipal water supply systems that are extremely reliable and largely invisible to the average person. These systems supply over 264 million Americans with a seemingly endless supply of sparkling freshwater for drinking, showering, cleaning, cooking, and other uses. The water is delivered through more than 1 million miles (1.6 million km) of water mains, tunnels, and aqueducts—enough to twice stretch to the moon and back.

Water quality in the United States is regulated by the Environmental Protection Agency (EPA), which enforces regulations spelled out in a law called the Safe Drinking Water Act (SDWA) of 1974. At the time of the law's passage, one-third of all tap water in the United States contained unsafe levels of toxic industrial chemicals such as benzene, dioxin, and pesticides. When the SDWA went into effect, factories were required to use what the EPA called the best available technology to limit or eliminate pollution discharges into freshwater. The SDWA also required municipal water facilities to add new equipment that could filter out pollutants where possible.

Because of the SDWA, water utilities are obliged to test drinking water for contaminants and publish an annual *Consumer Confidence Report*, also known as an annual drinking water quality report. This publicly available report identifies the level of pollutants in drinking water and explains their possible health impacts.

On the fortieth anniversary of the SDWA in 2014, EPA administrator Gina McCarthy stated that "more than 90 percent of water customers enjoy drinking water that meets all standards all the time."[6] Because of these standards, most tap water is as clean—or cleaner—than bottled water. (The SDWA does not regulate bottled water.) Tap water is also much cheaper than bottled water. In 2015 the average American paid $2.50 for 600 gallons (2,271 L) of municipal water. This was equal to the cost of 1 gallon (3.8 L) of water purchased at the grocery store. The typical American uses 100 gallons (379 L) of water a day for drinking, bathing, flushing toilets, watering plants, and other uses. This means an individual

Treating Wastewater

Municipal water systems supply clean water for homes and businesses. A second part of that system transports dirty water to wastewater treatment facilities after it goes down the drain or is flushed down the toilet. Like water treatment facilities, wastewater operations, called sanitary sewer systems, are largely out of sight and out of mind. But these facilities are very important. Sewage is processed to remove contaminants such as human waste, bacteria, soap, and chemicals. Sewage treatment plants turn wastewater into water that is clean enough to be released back into rivers, lakes, aquifers, or the ocean.

When wastewater is created in homes and businesses, it flows from individual drains into sewers that transport it to a municipal facility. The water passes through a large screen made of bars that removes sticks, plastic, rags, and other large objects. The wastewater is transferred to settling tanks, where about three-quarters of the solids sink to the bottom within a few hours. Bacteria is added to the wastewater and breaks down about 85 percent of organic material into harmless by-products. Then chlorine, which kills 99 percent of the harmful bacteria and reduces odor, is added to the water. A process called dechlorination removes the chlorine from the water, which is then released back into the environment.

pays an average of $12 a month for tap water. Even though water companies across the nation are raising rates around 5 percent a year, freshwater remains an amazing bargain.

Pumping Water ■

Because it is plentiful and cheap, few people think about where their water comes from. But a consumer's tap is the endpoint of a long, complex system that contains three major components. Pumping stations extract water from rivers, lakes, and aquifers. Water is then transferred to treatment facilities, where impurities and pollutants are removed. The clean water is then pumped into the distribution system, which is the network of tunnels, aqueducts, and water mains that brings water to homes and businesses.

Pumping stations are the most visible component of the water system. They are aboveground and are usually located next to rivers, lakes, and reservoirs. By necessity, pumping stations are large facilities because water is heavy: a single gallon (3.8 L) weighs 8 pounds (3.6 kg). Pumps that move that much weight through pipes and aqueducts use a lot of electricity; water pumps consume around 10 percent of the world's energy supply. In California, the Edmonston Pumping Plant, south of Bakersfield, is the most powerful water pumping facility in the world—and the largest consumer of electricity in the state.

The Edmonston plant is part of the 444-mile-long (715 km) California Aqueduct, which begins at the Sacramento River delta east of San Francisco. The aqueduct delivers water to the 20 million people living in central and Southern California. In what engineers at the Edmonston plant call the Big Lift, the facility uses fourteen motor pumps that stand 65 feet (20 m) high and weigh 420 tons (381 t). The pumps raise the water 1,926 feet (587 m)

The California Aqueduct (a portion of which is pictured here) carries water to 20 million people living in central and Southern California. The aqueduct begins in Northern California at the Sacramento River delta and extends for more than four hundred miles.

up the side of the Tehachapi Mountains and push it into a series of tunnels and pipes that transport it west. After the Big Lift, it is all downhill for the huge column of water that fills reservoirs in and around Los Angeles. Moving water to this arid region comes at a price: the energy used annually by the Edmonston Pumping Plant is equal to the electricity consumed by all residences in Los Angeles. Despite energy expenditures, average Los Angeles residents only paid around $4.75 for 750 gallons (2,839 L) of water in 2016.

Making Water Palatable and Potable ■

The water treatment facilities that make up the second stage of the water supply chain ensure that water is palatable (pleasant tasting) and potable (safe to drink). The water treatment procedure begins when water is pumped from freshwater sources into the plant. Screens made of thick steel bars about 2 inches (5 cm) apart prevent fish, branches, brush, and other large objects from entering the facility's intake pipes. A series of smaller screens removes twigs and leaves. Water that is turbid, or cloudy and muddy, is held in what is called a presedimentation basin. As the water sits in the basin, sand and soil naturally settle to the bottom.

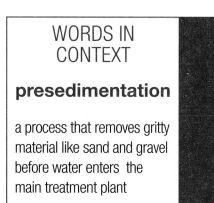

WORDS IN CONTEXT

presedimentation

a process that removes gritty material like sand and gravel before water enters the main treatment plant

After the presedimentation process, tiny particles such as dirt and aquatic organisms called algae remain in the water. These are removed through a method called coagulation, in which the chemical alum is added to the water. Alum causes a chemical reaction that forces particles to clump together, or coagulate, into a jelly-like mass that can be filtered out. Another chemical, powdered activated carbon, might also be added during the coagulation process. This chemical absorbs bacteria and other substances that can cause foul odors and unpleasant flavors in the water.

Balancing Acid and Alkaline ■

Water treatment facilities often add chemicals to balance what is called the pH value of the water. The pH of a solution determines its level of acidity or alkalinity on a scale of 1 to 14. Low pH values around 1 or 2 indicate a solution that is as acidic as lemon juice. Acidic water is highly corrosive. It is unhealthy to drink and destroys metal pipes that are part of the water distribution system. A high pH value of 12 or 13 indicates a solution as alkaline as ammonia or lye. Highly alkaline water is also unhealthy and produces an unpleasant taste.

The pH of water is affected by natural conditions such as the types of minerals found in local rocks where water is drawn. For example, limestone makes groundwater more alkaline. Water can become too acidic due to acid rain. This type of rain is caused by emissions from coal-burning power plants that release acidic chemicals such as sulfur dioxide into the air.

WORDS IN CONTEXT

alkalinity

a measure of a material's ability to neutralize acids

The normal pH range for drinking water is 6 to 8.5—with 7 being neutral (neither acidic nor alkaline). If water is acidic, treatment facilities add soda ash (sodium carbonate) and sodium hydroxide to raise the pH to neutral. If water is too alkaline, white vinegar or citric acid is added to balance the pH.

Once chemicals are introduced, the water is gently stirred for around thirty minutes. The water is then transferred to a sedimentation basin for three hours. This process allows whatever coagulated particles that remain in the water to sink to the bottom. The water is then filtered through a bed of sand that is around 2 feet (0.6 m) thick. (The sand sits on top of a bed of gravel and does not leach into the water.) This process removes remaining microscopic particles from the water.

In the final stage of the process, water is disinfected with chlorine—a chemical that kills microorganisms such as bacteria and viruses that can be found in reservoirs, water storage tanks, and water mains. These microorganisms can transmit diseases such as cholera, typhoid fever, dysentery, hepatitis, meningitis, and numerous other maladies that cause fever, vomiting, muscle aches, severe stomach and intestinal problems, and death. In about 75 percent of community water systems in the United States, the chemical fluoride—which protects against dental cavities—is also added in the final stage of water processing. The final product is pumped into pipes for transport to homes and businesses.

Quenching Thirst with Sachets ■

Most industrialized nations have advanced water delivery systems with stringent standards for drinking water quality. This is not the case in Africa, however, where the majority of people do not have easy access to clean water. In sub-Saharan Africa (the area of the continent located south of the Sahara Desert) only 16 percent of

The Struggle to Find Water in Ghana

Millions of people in Accra, Ghana, must buy water for drinking, bathing, and washing dishes. This source of purchased water, commonly known as a Kufuor gallon, is sold in 5.2-gallon (20 L) yellow plastic containers that once held cooking oil. Kufuor gallons are named after John Agyekum Kufuor, the president of Ghana from 2001 to 2009—ironically, a period of extensive water shortages. Kufuor gallons are often produced by the 10 percent of Accra residents who have access to tap water. And the yellow containers are ubiquitous, sold in shops, marketplaces, and on city streets in Accra.

According to the UN, every adult needs about 13 gallons (49 L) of water per day to drink, prepare meals, and maintain personal hygiene. That amount equals two and a half Kufuor gallons. Since a Kufuor gallon weighs over 42 pounds (19 kg), each individual needs to haul 105 pounds (48 kg) of water a day for personal use. In addition to being heavy, Kufuor gallons are expensive; each one sells for around 30 cents. This might not seem like much to a Westerner, but the average person in Ghana makes around thirty-eight dollars a week. This means a typical Ghanaian can spend more than 25 percent of his or her income on water. Artist Serge Attukwei Clottey, who makes art from worn-out Kufuor gallon containers, comments on the situation: "Any time you see yellow, it represents water. And any time you see the gallon, it represents struggle."

Quoted in Shaun Raviv, "The Cost of Pure Water," *Mosaic*, April 14, 2015. https://mosaicscience.com.

people receive their water from municipal water systems, and most of these people are wealthy. This leaves many urban Africans to rely on expensive water delivered to neighborhoods by tank trucks.

The complexities of delivering potable water to large populations can be seen in the West African Republic of Ghana. Ghana's capital city, Accra, is the commercial hub of West Africa. However, there are only two water treatment plants for the city's 6 million residents. (By contrast, Philadelphia has two water treatment plants serving 1.5 million inhabitants.) The Accra facilities are old and unreliable; major pipes often crack, and equipment breakdowns are common. This means that Accra's network of municipal water pipes can only deliver poor-quality water to city taps about half the time. And 90 percent of city residents are not even connected to the system; they haul around 5.2-gallon (20 L) containers called Kufuor gallons that they fill with expensive purchased water.

The chronic shortage of water in Accra has left it to entrepreneurs to fill in the gaps. One of those entrepreneurs, John Afele, calls himself "Johnny Water." He has a specially designed machine that fills sandwich bag–sized plastic sleeves called sachets with filtered well water. Each sachet holds 17 ounces (503 mL) of water. His machine can produce two thousand sachets per hour. It sterilizes the water using ultraviolet light to kill harmful bacteria. Each bag is heat sealed so no glues or sealants contaminate the water. Sachet producers can label each bag with a date and logo. Consumers drink the water by biting off the corner of the bag and gently squeezing the water into their mouths.

The sachet business has become a growing cottage industry in Accra. About 70 percent of water sachets are made by small operators like Johnny Water. However, in recent years large corporations like the bottled water company Voltic and the beer maker SABMiller have started to compete with the individual operators.

Regardless of who sells them, the sachets have provided a huge economic boost in a poor nation. Water sachets are sold out of ice-packed coolers on street corners, at roadside shops, and from three-wheeled carts and flatbed trucks. People stuck in Accra's notoriously traffic-snarled streets see a nonstop parade of women and girls who sing out "PURE-water!"[7] as they sell chilled sachets from pans balanced on their heads. These vendors can make around five dollars a day, which is the daily average wage for people in Ghana.

A resident of Accra in the African nation of Ghana carries water sachets to sell. Because Accra is chronically short of water, residents typically buy filtered well water in these sandwich bag–sized plastic sleeves called sachets.

American journalist Sharon Benzoni, who worked as an Accra-based blogger in 2014, describes her reaction to the sachet phenomenon: "Though I was wary of drinking water from a plastic bag when I first encountered it, at five cents a sachet, pure water quickly became my own go-to beverage as well. Bottled water is twenty to thirty times as expensive, making pure water an obvious choice . . . to municipal water, which has [a] spotty reputation."[8]

That lack of trust in municipal water systems is common in other nations where the sachet water business is exploding. Grassroots operators are producing sachets in Nigeria, India, and parts of Central America. Although sachet water is generally safer than municipal water, there is a huge downside to the phenomenon: the little plastic bags are having a major environmental impact. Rivers are choked with discarded sachets, and the beaches around Accra are littered with the bags. Sachets also clog storm drains and cause flooding. This results, ironically, in the spread of waterborne diseases.

Is It Safe to Drink? ■

Sachet water has not yet appeared in China, but it probably will in coming years. Most major Chinese municipalities have water treatment plants, but the tap water in China is particularly bad. Disease-causing microbes grow freely in the old metal pipes, pumps, and other municipal water supply infrastructure. Additionally, many water sources are extremely polluted. This makes Chinese tap water undrinkable—and it cannot be used for brushing teeth or washing fruits and vegetables. For these reasons, almost everyone in China relies on bottled water for drinking. Those who cannot afford bottled water boil their tap water before they drink it. Although boiling does not reduce pollution levels, it does kill deadly microorganisms.

Western visitors to China and other developing nations often ask, "Is it safe to drink the water?"[9] In many countries the answer is absolutely not; a citizen of Accra who purchases expensive water every day would gladly trade places with the American who pours gallons of pure water down the sink without a thought. Even though most people in industrialized nations rarely think about the water that flows from their taps, they should consider themselves lucky. They live in places where engineers have ensured that inexpensive drinking water is readily available every hour of every day of the year.

WORDS IN CONTEXT

infrastructure

the basic physical structures and facilities, such as roads, aqueducts, water pipes, sewers, and power plants, needed for the operation of a society

CHAPTER 2

PROBLEMS: Pollution, Waste, and Drought

"Numerous [water] systems across the country have tested with high lead levels over and over again, which raises concerns about what may be going on [with people's health] in those communities."

—Alison Young, investigative journalist

Quoted in Adam Wernick, "An Investigation Has Found Lead in 2,000 Water Systems," PRI, April 9, 2016. www.pri.org.

Clean water is one of the most precious resources on Earth. But this precious resource is under constant attack. On a single day in October 2016, news stories described Iowa drinking water contaminated by agricultural chemicals, Wisconsin drinking water containing toxic industrial chemicals, and Missouri drinking water fouled with dangerous levels of bacteria from sewage. And problems exist in nearly every city and state. According to a 2016 study by the advocacy organization Environmental Working Group, the cancer-causing chemical chromium-6 is present in municipal water systems across America. Chromium-6, which is used in a variety of industrial processes, can be found in dangerous levels in drinking water consumed by 218 million Americans—two-thirds of the population.

Pollution from Many Sources ■

Chromium-6 is released into the environment through leaky storage tanks, poor handling procedures, and inadequate waste disposal practices. It is among hundreds of toxic chemicals found in water supplies. Like chromium-6, many of these toxins are known as nonpoint source pollution—they enter the environment from numerous sources rather than a single source like a factory. Nonpoint source pollution includes motor oil, gasoline, antifreeze, and other automotive chemicals. Other sources of nonpoint source pollution include fertilizers, herbicides, and pesticides from farms and chemicals that leak from mining and oil-drilling operations. All of these pollutants seep into aquifers and wash into rivers, lakes, and streams when it rains or snows. Since nonpoint source pollution comes from such a broad range of sources, control measures to keep the toxins out of drinking water are extremely difficult and expensive to implement.

The problem of toxic chemicals in the water supply is not confined to any one nation. In China many freshwater sources are heavily polluted with agricultural and industrial chemicals. China's Environmental Ministry reported in 2015 that 60 percent of the country's aquifers—and one-third of its surface waters—are unfit for drinking or bathing.

Millions of people who live in rural areas without access to bottled water have little choice but to use the tainted water to drink, cook, clean, and water crops. And this is cause for concern. According to a Chinese environmental scientist known only as Qiu J, 190 million people in China become ill and 60,000 die from diseases caused by water pollution every year. Many victims of Chinese water pollution live in places known as cancer villages, where people suffer unnaturally high rates of cancer due to factory waste that is dumped into local water supplies.

Leaching Lead in Flint ■

Chromium-6 is a heavy metal, a substance with an atomic weight five times that of water. Other heavy metals include gold, arsenic, mercury, and silver. These substances occur naturally in the environment, and small amounts of some heavy metals, such as chromium, copper, selenium, and zinc, are essential to the metabolism of the human body. However, at high concentrations heavy metals are poisonous; exposure to heavy metals can damage the nerves, lungs, kidneys, liver, bones, and glands.

Lead is a heavy metal that is particularly harmful to the developing brains of young children. According to the World Health Organization, lead toxicity can cause irreversible learning disabilities, behavioral problems, and loss of intellectual abilities as measured by intelligence quotient, or IQ, tests. Lead exposure can also re-

A resident of Flint, Michigan, displays water samples from her home in 2015. Flint's water supply was found to contain unsafe levels of lead after officials switched to a new water source to save money.

sult in high blood pressure, heart and kidney disease, and reproductive problems in women. Perhaps the most troublesome aspect of lead exposure is that the metal is delivered to water taps through tainted pipes throughout the country. This issue made headlines in 2015 when people in Flint, Michigan, began showing signs of lead poisoning.

As in many Midwestern cities, most of Flint's water pipes were laid in the early 1900s and had not been upgraded since that time. It was common during that era for most water pipes to be made from two types of material: lead and cast iron. Lead is a relatively soft material that made the pipes easy to cut and shape when they were installed in individual homes. Flint's lead and cast iron water pipes worked well for decades. This is because the Detroit Water and Sewage Department (DWSD), which supplied the city's water from Lake Huron and the Detroit River, added a chemical called orthophosphate to the water. Orthophosphate prevents corrosion in pipes by forming a protective film that stops lead and rust from leaching into the water.

WORDS IN CONTEXT

orthophosphate

a chemical that prevents corrosion in pipes so that lead and rust do not leach into drinking water

Flint is a majority black city where 40 percent of the residents live in poverty and government administrators often struggle with budget shortfalls. In 2014 Flint officials decided to switch to a new water source after the DWSD increased its rates. City officials started up the local water treatment plant, which had been idle for decades, and began drawing water from the Flint River on April 25, 2014. That day Flint's mayor, Dayne Walling, issued a press release: "It's regular, good, pure drinking water, and it's right in our backyard."[10]

Losing IQ Points ◼

Despite Walling's assurance, many of Flint's one hundred thousand residents immediately noticed the new water was bad. As Flint resident Melissa Mays stated, "After the water switch, I ran the kitchen tap and it came out just yellow, just disgusting yellow."[11] Mays and her neighbors could see there was a problem, but few of them knew the reason. It was later discovered that the Flint water department did not add orthophosphate. This made Flint tap water much more acidic and caused the protective coating that had been forming in the pipes for decades to dissolve. As investigative reporter Alison Young explains, the Flint water "basically stripped the insides of pipes and sent torrents of particles and lead into people's homes."[12] These particles colored the water a murky yellowish brown while newly released bacteria made it foamy and gave it a rotten-egg smell.

Flint residents complained for months, but city and state environmental officials denied there was any problem. Even when tests revealed high lead levels in the drinking water, officials downplayed the hazards. As a nurse employed by the state told a young mother who was worried about the high levels of lead in her child's blood, "[He'll only lose] a few IQ points. . . . It is not the end of the world."[13]

The seriousness of the problem was highlighted in early 2015 when a research team from Virginia Tech traveled to Flint to thoroughly test the tap water. Lead is measured in parts per billion (ppb), and EPA regulations state that water with more than 15 ppb of lead is unsafe. The Virginia Tech researchers were startled by what they found at the home of LeeAnne Walters: her tap water contained 397 ppb of lead. Walters was the mother of four, and her children suffered from numerous maladies caused by the contaminated water flowing from her taps. Her three-year-old twins suffered from painful burning rashes, and one of the twins had stopped growing. Her fourteen-year-old was stricken with abdominal cramps so severe that she required several trips to the emergency room. Walters also had problems; at one point her

Chromium-6: An Unregulated Chemical

The EPA has known about the health hazards of chromium-6 for decades. The chemical made headlines in the late 1990s when environmental activist Erin Brockovich revealed that the utility company Pacific Gas & Electric (PG&E) had been leaking the chemical into the groundwater supply of Hinkley, California, for thirty years. Many of the town's six hundred residents were afflicted by stomach cancer, liver damage, and reproductive problems.

Brockovich's battle with PG&E was brought to the public's attention in the 2000 movie *Erin Brockovich* starring Julia Roberts. However, the EPA never set regulations to prevent chromium-6 from leaching into drinking water supplies. In 2016 Brockovich made note of this problem:

> More than 20 years ago, we learned that this dangerous chemical poisoned the tap water of California communities. . . . But in that time the EPA hasn't set drinking water standards for . . . chromium-6. This is an abject failure by the EPA, including members of Congress charged with overseeing the agency, and every American should be outraged by this inaction.

Quoted in Pam Wright, "'Erin Brockovich' Chemical Taints Tap Water of 218 Million Americans, Study Finds," Weather Channel, September 22, 2016. https://weather.com.

eyelashes fell out. All of these problems were later blamed on the long-term effects of lead poisoning.

In October 2015 Flint switched back to the Detroit water supply, but it was too late. Corrosion in the pipes continued to taint the water supply. In January 2016 President Barack Obama declared a state of emergency in Flint. This allowed the Federal Emergency Management Agency to provide Flint residents with bottled water, water filters for their homes, test kits, and other equipment. Five Michigan government officials resigned or were fired over the mishandling of the crisis; three faced criminal charges for covering up the problem. Studies conducted in late 2016 showed that around twelve thousand Flint children were exposed to high levels of lead and would face serious health problems. Several lawsuits were filed against the state and city, and Michigan is now spending more than $165 million to replace the city's water pipes. Ironically, the switch to Flint River water was done to save the city $5 million a year.

The Challenge of Water Inequality ■

The issue of lead in water pipes extends far beyond the problems in Flint. Thousands of cities installed lead water pipes until the substance was banned from water systems in 1986. As a result, forty-one states have unsafe levels of lead in their water supply, according to a 2016 EPA report. Elevated levels of lead were also found in numerous city water supplies, including those in San Francisco, Philadelphia, Seattle, and Washington, DC. The EPA said that water being supplied to at least seven thousand schools has more than 15 ppb of lead.

On March 22, 2016, Obama pledged to improve drinking water quality in the United States. March 22 is acknowledged by the UN as World Water Day, when people can show they care about water quality and supply. According to a White House press release on World Water Day,

> Water challenges are facing communities and regions across the United States, impacting millions of lives and costing billions of dollars in damages. These challenges are particularly problematic in predominantly poor, minority, or rural communities, where water inequality can go

hand-in-hand with socioeconomic inequality. . . . Accordingly, we must work together to build a sustainable water future—one in which everyone has access to the safe, clean, and affordable water they need, when and where they need it.[14]

The announcement included plans to invest $5 billion on water infrastructure projects nationwide. However, the EPA estimates it would cost $275 billion to make all of America's water infrastructure lead free.

Down the Drain ■

Although lead in pipes is a serious problem, the aging water infrastructure is also wasting huge amounts of water due to leaky pipes, faucets, and aqueducts. Every day in the United States, 7 billion gallons (26.4 billion L) of clean drinking water goes down the drain from leaking household faucets. City water systems are another source of wasted water. According to the American Society of Civil Engineers, an organization that designs, constructs, and studies water systems and other infrastructure, there are

Leaking household faucets are to blame for billions of gallons of wasted water. Water main breaks are another source of waste.

China's Cancer Villages

China is one of the largest manufacturing nations in the world. The country's factories produce electronics, clothing, and nearly every other product found in stores throughout the world. Although China's industrialization has helped lift millions of its citizens out of poverty, the growth has taken a toll on the environment. Many of China's rivers turn unnatural shades of orange, green, and even bloodred due to toxic chemicals spewing from factory drainpipes. This has given rise to a new name for small communities in China: cancer villages. These are places where cancer rates have soared above the national average. The villages are located on riverbanks near polluting power plants, paper-making and textile factories, pharmaceutical manufacturers, and chemical plants. According to various reports in the Chinese media, there are 459 cancer villages spread throughout the country.

Most of China's major factories have been constructed since the early 2000s. They sprang up near fishing villages in rural China where residents had been drinking water from the river for centuries. Villagers continued with their traditional lifestyles as the rivers they depended on rapidly changed into industrial sewers. Soon they began to suffer from unnaturally high rates of cancer. Despite China's laws against polluting waterways, factory owners bribed officials to ignore the problem. It was not until 2013 that the government officially acknowledged the existence of cancer villages. Although some of the most egregious polluters have been shut down, the toxins they dumped in the water will continue to sicken villagers for decades.

an estimated 240,000 water main breaks per year in the United States. Together, these breaks waste billions of gallons of drinking water annually. And the bigger the city, the bigger the leaks; New York City's water delivery system loses water on a massive scale. The Delaware Aqueduct, which provides about 65 percent of the city's daily water needs, is a good example.

The Delaware Aqueduct was built between 1937 and 1945, and it has been leaking since at least the late 1980s. Every day an estimated 35 million gallons (132 million L) of freshwater—enough water every day to supply the needs of 350,000 Americans—

leaks out of the aqueduct. New York City officials have spent decades trying to address the problems, which are both complicated and expensive. It was finally decided that a $1.5 billion tunnel was needed to bypass the leakiest sections of the aqueduct. The project, which began in 2010, is planned for completion sometime after 2021. When completed, the old sections will be sealed with concrete and abandoned.

Developing nations lack money and the political will to address the issue of water waste. The water infrastructure in most African cities like Lagos, Nigeria, and Nairobi, Kenya, is old, leaky, and poorly maintained. And even these inferior systems are unavailable to the vast majority of Africans who live in overcrowded slums. Most rural areas of Africa also lack water and sewer lines. Without water delivery systems, many Africans either collect water from polluted streams and lakes, buy their water from private sellers, or get water from outdoor public pipes. The outdoor pipes, with taps for dispensing water, are often filthy and poorly maintained. And the job of waiting in line for water, filling up jugs, and hauling them long distances falls to women and girls. In Kenya it is common for women to walk six hours a day to find water for their families. With so much of the female population dealing with this tedious chore, there is little time to earn a living or attend school, keeping the women trapped in poverty. According to the UN, Africans spend a total of 40 billion working hours each year carrying water.

Not a Drop to Waste ■

According to the World Water Council policy institute, 1.1 billion people, mostly in developing nations, live without access to safe drinking water. And the problem is only going to get worse according to the results from a NASA research program. In 2015 a pair of twin research satellites referred to as GRACE (Gravity Recovery and Climate Experiment) completed an eleven-year study of the thirty-seven largest aquifers on Earth. By measuring the pull of gravity over the aquifers, NASA was able to determine how much water was being used. (When the amount of water in an aquifer decreases, so does the pull of gravity over the aquifer.)

A central California farmworker picks and packages raspberries. The state's large agricultural regions and its populous urban areas both rely on California's Central Valley aquifer, which is threatened by a long-running statewide drought.

The NASA study revealed that one-third of the underground water deposits were being used at an unsustainable rate. The twenty-one aquifers were considered by NASA to be stressed—a term that means water was being consumed faster than it could be replenished by rainfall and snowmelt. Out of these aquifers, five were extremely or highly stressed; the aquifers were in trouble but had some water flowing back into them. Another eight aquifers were listed as overstressed because there was no natural replenishment of the groundwater.

California's Central Valley aquifer system was one of those that NASA listed as extremely stressed. The aquifer contains water that seeped into the ground around twenty thousand years ago, and it provides almost half of all water consumed by California's 39 million people. The aquifer is also critical to farmers who grow crops on more than a million acres in the Central Valley, an agricultural region that runs through the center of the state. At the time the NASA study was released, California had been suffering through a prolonged, six-year drought.

As the aquifer drains, the land above it is sinking at a rate of 6 inches (15 cm) per year in some places. When the land sinks down into the aquifer, it reduces the original size of the underground reservoir. If or when the rains return to California, the aquifers will be smaller, unable to hold as much water as they once did.

The NASA study showed that the Arabian aquifer system was the most dangerously stressed. This aquifer, which provides water to more than 60 million people in nations including Israel, Palestine, Jordan, Lebanon, and Syria, was not being replenished at all. The environment of the Middle East is traditionally very arid, but NASA reported that as of 2015 the region was suffering the worst drought in over nine hundred years.

Other stressed aquifers were found in Europe, parts of Africa and Asia, and Australia. Alexandra Richey, who directed the NASA study, is alarmed: "We know we're taking more [water from aquifers] than we're putting back in—how long do we have before we can't do that anymore? We don't know, but we keep pumping, which to me is terrifying."[15]

WORDS IN CONTEXT

unsustainable

not able to be maintained at the current rate or level

NASA reports that the historic droughts are caused by climate change. Add in other human-made calamities, such as pollution of water sources and toxic water delivery systems, and the scope of the problem touches nearly everyone on Earth. In the twenty-first century a new generation of engineers is needed to correct some of these problems and point a way forward into a new era where technology can reverse the damage done in the past.

CHAPTER 3

SOLUTIONS: Transforming Seawater to Freshwater

"Advancements [in desalination] will continue but improvements will always be about the bottom line, making it cheaper and more economical to use. It can only get cheaper and more efficient at this point. . . . There is no turning back the tide now."

—Stanley Weiner, promoter of next-generation desalination technology

Quoted in James Stafford, "The Game-Changing Water Revolution: Interview with Stanley Weiner," OilPrice .com, April 13, 2015. http://oilprice.com.

Freshwater resources make up only a tiny percentage of all water on Earth. But there is enough water in the ocean to forever quench humanity's thirst while providing ample water for agriculture and industry. There is one obvious complication: the salt must first be removed before ocean water can be made potable. And removing salt from water using current methods requires a lot of energy and expensive technology. These limitations have prevented desalinated ocean water from freely flowing into millions of taps and farm fields throughout the world.

But scientists and engineers have been working on making desalination technology less costly and more efficient. One way of accomplishing this is to use solar power rather than fossil fuels to generate the electricity that powers the desalination process. Nanotechnology is another promising option. Filters made from tiny nanotubes remove a much higher percentage of salt from seawater than present-day filters, which were invented during the last century. Engineers are also working to develop small-scale desalination equipment, mobile facilities that are easy to move around and set up where needed. A Dutch company called Salttech has developed highly efficient desalination technology that fits into stackable shipping containers—steel boxes like those seen on big eighteen-wheeler trucks. These modular units can be purchased for a fraction of the cost of a centralized billion-dollar desalination plant. For example, a solar-powered Salttech pilot project in Mentone, Texas, which went online in 2015, cost $3.5 million and provides drinking water from a salty aquifer located beneath the small town.

The new desalination technology has the ability to solve freshwater problems in landlocked regions like Mentone and is becoming increasingly important in cities situated near the ocean. As Salttech spokesman Stanley Weiner states, "This is a revolution, and it's only just emerging, so we can expect a lot of technological advancements along the way to make desalination even more efficient and cost-effective."[16]

Evaporated Water ■

In 2016 there were more than 18,400 desalination plants operating worldwide, according to the International Desalination Association trade group. These facilities provided freshwater to around 300 million people in 150 nations. But basic desalination has been practiced for centuries using a heat-based process called thermal desalination. When salt water is heated, it evaporates into water vapor in the form of steam. As the steam rises, it is collected, cooled, and condensed back into drinking water, while the salt is left behind in the boiler. The process is similar to how rain is created: the sun heats and evaporates surface water, which at the same time is separated from salt, dirt, minerals, and other matter. When the water vapor rises, the molecules cool, re-form, and return to liquid in the form of rain. This natural process is why rainwater is safe to drink almost everywhere in the world (before it hits the ground). Journalist Steven Solomon eloquently explains the natural process: "Evaporated water precipitates in a desalinated and cleansed form over the planet through Earth's continuous water cycle to restore natural ecosystems and make sustained human civilization possible."[17]

Thermal desalination, which mimics nature, allowed early sailors to travel vast distances across the ocean. During the sixteenth century most ships had boilers for thermal desalination

A desalination plant in Germany (pictured) is one of thousands operating worldwide. Homes and businesses in about 150 countries use desalinated water on a daily basis.

that produced drinking water for crews. This form of desalination remained a feature of shipboard life until the 1950s. However, a substantial amount of energy is required to boil water for thermal desalination. This makes the process impractical except in locations where cheap energy is abundant. For example, in Saudi Arabia, Kuwait, and Qatar, water is scarce, but oil is plentiful. Thermal seawater desalination has been practiced on a large scale for more than sixty years in these oil-rich nations, and it remains the prevailing desalting technology in the twenty-first century.

Reverse Osmosis ■

A different method for desalination was introduced in 1956 when researchers at the University of California–Los Angeles, created a filter from a synthetic fiber called cellulose acetate. Cellulose acetate, which is commonly used for cigarette filters, is known as a semipermeable membrane; it has billions of tiny holes that allow some atoms and molecules to pass through it but not others. A cellulose acetate membrane might be compared to a screen door that contains holes large enough to allow air to pass through but small enough to prevent insects from entering the home. When seawater is pushed through a semipermeable membrane, it blocks the passage of larger salt molecules while allowing smaller water molecules to pass through. By the late 1950s cellulose acetate filters were being used in a new desalination process known as reverse osmosis (RO). In simple terms, the RO process involves forcing seawater through a semipermeable membrane to remove up to 99 percent of the salt.

Engineers created RO based on a naturally occurring process called osmosis in which fluids, called solutions, flow through a semipermeable membrane. When the two solutions are freshwater and seawater, the freshwater is naturally drawn through the membrane toward the seawater. This process occurs because saltwater is a more concentrated solution; it contains molecules of dissolved salt that make it heavier and denser than freshwater. Scientists say freshwater is a weaker solution. With osmosis, a weaker solution will always flow through a semipermeable membrane toward a more concentrated solution. Osmosis occurs frequently in nature with many types of liquids and substances. A good example of osmosis is when plant roots absorb water from the soil while filtering out sand, microbes, and other unwanted elements.

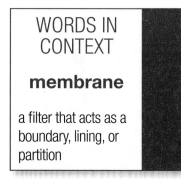

WORDS IN CONTEXT

membrane

a filter that acts as a boundary, lining, or partition

RO is the osmosis process in reverse—a more concentrated solution (seawater) flows through a membrane toward a weaker solution (freshwater). With RO, the semipermeable membrane filters out the salt in seawater as the liquid flows toward freshwater. But RO is not a natural process—high-pressure electric pumps are required to push the concentrated solution through the membrane into the weaker solution.

The first desalination facility in the United States to use RO on a large scale was opened in Coral Cape, Florida, in 1977. The plant was so successful that in 1985 it expanded to become the largest RO water purifying plant in the world. Over time better semipermeable membranes were developed, and new technology was put in place as RO desalination plants were built

Many desalination plants use reverse osmosis to transform saltwater into drinkable water. The basis of reverse osmosis is osmosis, a naturally occuring process in which low-salt solutions naturally flow toward high-salt solutions. This is how plant roots absorb water from soil, for instance.

Osmosis

How osmosis works:
A semipermeable membrane separates two containers. One container holds water with a low level of salt. The other holds water with a high concentration of salt. During osmosis, the low-salt water will naturally flow toward the saltier liquid. The membrane will allow salt but not water molecules to pass through to the other container—leaving freshwater behind.

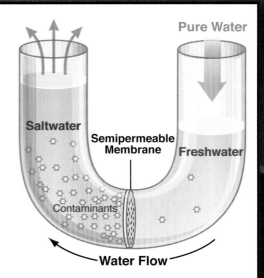

Reverse Osmosis

How reverse osmosis works:
The same two containers are again separated by a semi-permeable membrane. But this time, pressure is applied to the container that holds the salty water. The pressure forces the water molecules through the membrane in the reverse (or opposite) direction while at the same time preventing most salt and other contaminants from slipping through.

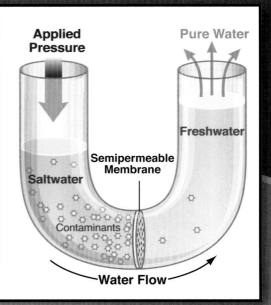

Source: Puretec Industrial Water, "What Is Reverse Osmosis?." http://puretecwater.com.

throughout the world. About 70 percent of the desalination plants currently use the RO process. Because it is a time-tested technology, and more energy efficient than thermal desalination, RO is the preferred filtering method for most new facilities.

The Fish-Kill Problem ■

Desalination plants—no matter what type of technology they utilize—can have a negative impact on the marine environment. One major problem occurs when huge volumes of seawater are drawn into a desalination facility through large pipes located in the ocean, a process called direct intake. During the direct intake process, seawater passes through a screen to prevent objects and debris from being pulled into the plant. Fish and other marine organisms like jellyfish and starfish die when they become trapped on the intake screens. Billions of smaller organisms, such as fish eggs and plankton, die during the RO process when the saltwater is filtered through the membrane.

The Carlsbad Desalination Plant, located north of San Diego, is working to solve the fish-kill problem. The plant, which opened in 2015, uses fish screens with tiny openings just 0.04 inches (1 mm) wide (about the thickness of a credit card). The screens strain out 95 percent of the fish before they are drawn into the intake pipe. However, this only accounts for 20 percent of all organisms sucked into the desalination plant; the remaining 80 percent—plankton and fish eggs—are destroyed by the RO membranes.

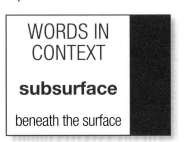

WORDS IN CONTEXT

subsurface

beneath the surface

Engineers are searching for new ways to eliminate the fish-kill problem caused by direct intake. A system called subsurface intake relies on various types of wells drilled near a shoreline or under the ocean floor. The seawater filters into the wells through layers of mud and sand that filter out fish, plankton, and other living organisms. However, subsurface intake systems are extremely complex and often are not practical; each well can only pull in a small amount of water compared to an open pipe. A typical desalination plant might require two hundred subsurface wells to supply its daily seawater needs. This makes subsurface systems far more expensive than direct intake; a subsurface system might represent up to 20 percent of a facility's total construction costs.

Salt Brine and Sea Life ■

Another major environmental problem associated with desalination concerns the salty muck, called brine, that is filtered out of the seawater. A typical desalination plant creates 1 gallon (3.8 L) of brine for every gallon of freshwater produced. For example, the Carlsbad plant pulls in 100 million gallons (378 million L) of water from the ocean daily to produce 50 million gallons (227 million L) of freshwater. The 50 million gallons of brine is discharged into the ocean.

Brine has twice the salt content of seawater. It is so salty that waves and tides, which would normally help flush and disperse impurities, do not dissolve it. The high concentration of salt in brine kills most living creatures that are exposed to it. Victoria Whitney, deputy director of California's state water board, explains that brine and seawater are "like oil and vinegar—they stay separate. You end up with these very large dead zones . . . where you have really salty water just sitting on the ocean bottom."[18] These large dead zones are devoid of all marine life.

Some of the brine problems can be alleviated by using spray nozzles to discharge the super-salty liquid underwater. This allows the brine to dissolve as it slowly mixes with seawater. Yet for the process to work, the brine must be sprayed using extreme pressure, comparable to water shooting out of a fire hose. This creates another problem: when sea creatures swim into the path of the highly pressurized brine spray, they are instantly killed.

Solar-Powered Desalination ■

Another problem with desalination is the cost. The facilities use a lot of power to filter seawater. As tech writer Brian Bienkowski writes, "Desalination is an . . . energy hog."[19] Desalination plants use from five to ten times more electricity than traditional metropolitan drinking water treatment plants. This makes desalinated water an expensive option: 1,000 gallons (3,785 L) of desalinated water cost around four dollars in 2015, about twice the cost of conventional freshwater. And, since most desalination plants depend on fossil fuels for their electricity, the process itself contributes to air pollution and climate change.

The problem of high energy consumption during the desalination process is being addressed in an unlikely place—Saudi Arabia. Saudi Arabia has the world's largest oil reserves; the country

Inexpensive and Compact Desalination Technology

In 2014 the Dutch company Salttech introduced game-changing desalination technology that is inexpensive, energy efficient, and not harmful to the environment. Salttech developed a desalination method called dynamic vapor recompression (DVR). It uses an evaporation process that takes place in a vacuum under high pressure, which separates freshwater from seawater. Heating water under high pressure requires much less energy than is used in the traditional thermal desalination process. With the DVR process, the briny water is not considered a waste product. Instead, it is transferred to a cyclonic separator, or cyclone, which spins very rapidly. The spinning separates the salt crystals from the water by centrifugal force. This process produces zero liquid discharge; the water can be used while solid salt is left behind. The salt can be recycled for use in manufacturing plastic, paper, glass, fertilizers, soaps, detergents, and dyes.

The DVR process is 97 percent efficient—only 3 percent of every gallon of freshwater produced is unusable. In addition to producing zero brine, DVR is solar powered and compact. The equipment can fit into shipping containers, which can be sent to seaside disaster zones where traditional drinking water facilities have been damaged by hurricanes or tornadoes. The equipment has also been deployed to small towns in Texas where drought has eliminated regional freshwater resources.

produces 10 million barrels of oil a day. Thus, the use of oil for power is not usually a problem for Saudi citizens. Many wealthy Saudis drive huge SUVs and keep their home air conditioners running even when they go on vacation. However, Saudi Arabia also burns around one-sixth of its oil every day to power twenty-eight desalination plants. Most of these plants use thermal desalination processes, pulling water from the Persian Gulf and the Red Sea to supply the kingdom with 70 percent of its water. Using all that crude oil to desalinate water is wasteful even by Saudi standards.

Concerns over wasteful oil consumption prompted Saudi leaders to commission the world's first large-scale RO desalination plant powered by solar energy. The $130 million plant, which was to go online in 2017, will supply freshwater to one hundred thousand people who live in the city of Al Khafji. But the solar-powered water facility is more than a way to create freshwater. Saudi leaders are looking for a way to diversify their nation's economy, which is reliant on oil exports. Rather than build the facility with so-called off-the-shelf equipment, or technology that was readily available, the Saudis decided to create a new industry. The Saudis are investing billions of their oil wealth to create and export clean, energy-efficient desalination technology.

Designing New Filters ■

In 2010 the Saudis embarked on a six-year research mission to develop a new type of RO filter. This was necessary because seawater in the Persian Gulf and Red Sea is about 5 percent saltier than ocean water found elsewhere. The high salinity is a result of the Saudi climate. Since it only rains about 3 inches (7.6 cm) a year, very little freshwater flows into the oceans that surround the country. Additionally, there is a very high water evaporation rate in a region where temperatures can reach 129°F (54°C). As the water evaporates from the ocean, salt is left behind. Pumping this high-salinity seawater through a regular semipermeable membrane requires more power than is used by a typical desalination plant.

> **WORDS IN CONTEXT**
>
> **semipermeable**
>
> allowing certain elements to pass through but not others

Working in collaboration with the American tech company IBM, the Saudis have developed a new type of RO membrane made from tiny structures called carbon nanotubes (CNTs). These tubular molecules, a thousand times thinner than a human hair, are incredibly strong for their size and weight. And carbon nanotube membranes are particularly efficient for use in desalination. Malaysian nanotech engineer Eaqub Ali explains: "The hollow pores of the CNTs are extremely, extremely tiny. However, because of their amazing chemical and physical properties, they allow frictionless [passing] of water through the pores, but reject most salts . . . and pollutants, giving us purified water, probably in its best form."[20] Carbon nanotubes are also resistant to mold, bacteria, and other toxic microbes that clog up traditional RO filters and reduce their efficiency.

A worker at a desalination plant in Saudi Arabia reviews a daily log. The Middle Eastern nation, which has far more oil than water, has devoted significant resources to desalination.

The goal of Saudi engineers is to produce an eco-friendly and cheap source of freshwater through the combination of carbon nanotube membranes and solar-powered desalination equipment. If the Al Khafji desalination facility works as planned, IBM predicts, the new technology will make freshwater so inexpensive that it will even become "economically feasible to produce water for agriculture."[21]

Reducing Brine ■

Although solar power and carbon nanotube filters might lower water production costs, the technology does little to reduce the amount of brine produced by the desalination process. The brine problem is the focus of California scientists at Humboldt State University and the University of Southern California. The researchers have developed a two-step method to reduce brine called reverse osmosis-pressure retarded osmosis (RO-PRO).

The complex concept behind RO-PRO is based on harvesting the energy generated during osmosis. The power is naturally created when freshwater passes through a membrane into saltwater on the other side. This process causes the water level on the salty side to rise. If the rising saltwater is in an enclosed tube, it creates pressure as it rises. This pressurized water can be directed to spin a rotating machine called a turbine, which creates power. This process is called pressure retarded osmosis. The power of the spinning turbine is directed to push seawater through the filter of the RO system. The brine that is left behind is diverted back for use in the first step of the process, so that it is diluted by freshwater. In addition to diluting the brine, the RO-PRO process uses 30 percent less energy than traditional RO systems.

WORDS IN CONTEXT

turbine

a machine to produce continuous power in which a wheel or rotor is made to revolve rapidly by a fast-moving flow of water, steam, gas, or air

In 2016 a prototype RO-PRO system was being tested on a small scale in the tiny Northern California town of Samoa. Humboldt State engineering professor Andrea Achilli explains the promise of RO-PRO: "If used on a large scale, it could have a positive environmental effect and result in significant cost and energy savings. . . . Eventually, we'd like to see the technology built into new desalination plants in California and elsewhere."[22]

Sustainable Water ■

Another energy-saving desalination process, still under development in 2017, is called forward osmosis. As with RO-PRO, the concept is complex. To understand forward osmosis, it is necessary to compare it to reverse osmosis. Forward osmosis and reverse osmosis both pass water through a semipermeable membrane. With reverse osmosis, seawater is pushed through the membrane under high pressure created by an electric pump. In forward osmosis, seawater is pulled—not pushed—through a membrane by what is called a draw solution. This draw solution is actually a saline gas made from ammonia and carbon dioxide that is mixed into freshwater. The gases give the draw solution a higher concentration of salt than seawater. This causes the seawater to flow into it at low pressure. After the water is pulled into the draw solution, it is heated. This releases the gas, which can be recycled back into the process. Freshwater is left behind.

Forward osmosis requires only 15 to 20 percent of the energy typically used in reverse osmosis desalination. This makes the process affordable anywhere desalinated water is needed. Ac-

Cleaning Up Farm Runoff

The new technology being developed for desalination can also be used to produce freshwater for agricultural purposes. A California company called WaterFX uses solar power to clean up the agricultural runoff that is a by-product of irrigation. This water is normally unusable because it contains salts and harmful chemicals used in pesticides and fertilizers.

In 2016 WaterFX began selling the Aqua4 concentrated solar still primarily for producing freshwater for use on California farms. The Aqua4 consists of twenty-four solar collectors that harness the power of the sun to create heat for its thermal desalination equipment. The unit can produce 65,000 gallons (246,052 L) of freshwater daily from the runoff. Because the system is solar powered, the freshwater it produces is 75 percent cheaper than desalinated water created through conventional methods. The brine that is a by-product of the process contains substances that can be recycled. For example, magnesium salts are used by the medical industry, and nitrogen is used to make gunpowder. WaterFX has plans to build at least ten solar desalination plants. According to WaterFX cofounder Aaron Mandell, "Eventually, if this all goes where I think it can, California could wind up with so much water it's able to export it instead of having to deal with shortages. What we are doing here is sustainable, scalable and affordable."

Quoted in Kevin Fagan, "California Drought: Solar Desalination Plant Shows Promise," SFGate, March 18, 2014. www.sfgate.com.

cording to an article on the process in *Yale Scientific,* "This new forward osmosis technology has the potential to cheaply and effectively promote a sustainable global water supply. . . . The new technology would serve a crucial function not only in developing but also in developed countries."[23]

In the coming decades, heavily populated nations will face mounting crises due to a scarcity of freshwater. But engineers have science on their side because freshwater can be separated from seawater by osmosis. By harnessing the sun, water pressure, and other natural forces, engineers will be a driving force behind a building boom of desalination plants everywhere salty waves lap upon the shore.

CHAPTER 4

SOLUTIONS:
Recycling Wastewater

"Every drop of water on the planet has been recycled at one time or another, but when you talk about bringing wastewater back to potable standards, people get a little squeamish."

—Sarah Fister Gale, water consultant

Sarah Fister Gale, "Battling Water Scarcity: Direct Potable Reuse Poised as Future of Water Recycling," *WaterWorld*, 2016. www.waterworld.com.

In 2016 one of the hottest new sources of drinking water in the United States was coming from an improbable place—sewage treatment plants. In drought-stricken states like California and Texas, water managers were starting to view wastewater as the new frontier of freshwater production.

Wastewater—the liquid that goes down toilets and drains—can be extensively treated, purified, and turned into sparkling-clean drinking water. As water expert Matt Weiser writes, "It is now possible to imagine a future in which highly treated wastewater will be plumbed directly into . . . homes as a new drinking water supply."[24] However, not everyone is as enthusiastic about the concept of turning wastewater into tap water. Opponents of wastewater recycling use the phrase "toilet to tap"[25] to describe the process. This phrase aptly captures the yuck factor—a view that water produced this way is somehow disgusting or contaminated.

The formal name for introducing treated wastewater directly into a municipal water supply is direct potable reuse (DPR). Whatever people might think of DPR, there is little doubt that new sources of water are needed as severe droughts increase in number. This is impacting economic activities and threatening water supplies. Since 2011, record droughts have hit the southeastern United States, the Midwest, and the West. In 2013 California experienced its driest year on record. In 2015 the state experienced its warmest year ever as drought conditions were seen in 75 percent of the state. And California was not alone; by 2016 Guatemala, Brazil, Puerto Rico, South Africa, Ethiopia, India, and parts of China were gripped by record-breaking droughts. These conditions were causing rivers and lakes to dry up, while aquifers were being drained faster than they could be recharged.

Although engineers cannot make it rain, they can use sophisticated technology to recycle wastewater. The first DPR plant in the United States opened in Big Spring, Texas, in 2013. The $14 million plant is operated by the Colorado River Municipal Water District, which supplies drinking water to 250,000 people in Big Spring and the nearby cities of Odessa, Snyder, and Midland. The water district plant, which produces up to 2 million gallons (7.5 million L) of freshwater every day, mixes one part DPR water with four parts water drawn from a local reservoir.

Big Spring water officials began planning the DPR plant in 2002, long before the historic drought hit Texas. As water district manager John Grant explains, "Looking 20 or 30 years down the road, we knew we wouldn't have any new lakes or surface reservoirs for water, so we started looking at alternate sources and technologies. Any great future project we [undertook would] likely involve advance [DPR] treatment."[26]

Although Big Spring had more than a decade to plan and build its DPR plant, water managers 240 miles (386 km) to the northeast in Wichita Falls, Texas, did not have that option. In 2012 Wichita Falls was facing a crisis: the city of 105,000 could run out of water within three years. Officials declared an emergency and installed DPR equipment in the local water treatment facility. They connected the facility to the Wichita Falls wastewater treatment plant with a 12-mile (19 km) pipeline and were producing DPR water within twenty-seven months. Faced with a civic disaster, Wichita Falls residents had no problem with the yuck factor. As Daniel Nix, the water utility operations manager, states, "The citizens wanted the DPR. They knew it was going to save them and they wanted it in a hurry."[27]

The contaminated water that flows down into toilets and drains can be treated and recycled and then added to a public water supply. This is known as direct potable reuse, or DPR. During the DPR process, wastewater collected by a reclamation plant undergoes three stringent stages of purification: microfiltration, reverse osmosis, and ultraviolet disinfection. It is during these stages that all impurities, bacteria, toxins, and any other contaminants are removed— with clean, drinkable water being the end result.

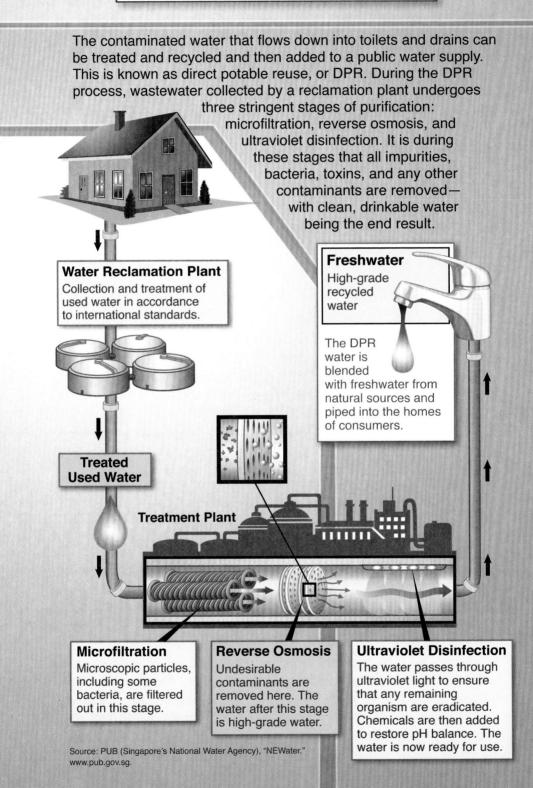

Water Reclamation Plant
Collection and treatment of used water in accordance to international standards.

Freshwater
High-grade recycled water

The DPR water is blended with freshwater from natural sources and piped into the homes of consumers.

Treated Used Water

Treatment Plant

Microfiltration
Microscopic particles, including some bacteria, are filtered out in this stage.

Reverse Osmosis
Undesirable contaminants are removed here. The water after this stage is high-grade water.

Ultraviolet Disinfection
The water passes through ultraviolet light to ensure that any remaining organism are eradicated. Chemicals are then added to restore pH balance. The water is now ready for use.

Source: PUB (Singapore's National Water Agency), "NEWater." www.pub.gov.sg.

High-Quality Water ■

The DPR process begins with water that goes down toilets and drains in homes and businesses. This wastewater, called effluent, is contaminated with human waste, soap, detergents, personal care products, and everything else that flows down the drain. Sewers carry effluent to wastewater treatment plants, where it is filtered and cleaned until it meets sufficient cleanup standards as defined in EPA regulations. This means that the treated effluent will not kill fish or other marine creatures when it is returned to waterways. The effluent must also be free from excessive nutrients like phosphorus and nitrogen, by-products of fertilizers and pet waste runoff that flow into sewers when it rains. These nutrients can cause rampant algae growth that will kill plants, fish, and other aquatic animals.

Treated effluent is nonpotable, or not fit for human consumption. When it is sent to a DPR facility, it undergoes further processing to make it potable. The first step in the DPR process is called microfiltration. The treated effluent is pumped through a microfilter, a membrane with tiny pores about 1/300th the width of a human hair. The microfilter removes solids, oils, and harmful bacteria that can cause serious health problems. The water next passes through an RO process to remove impurities such as grit, salts, and various other contaminants. The final step, called advanced oxidation process, exposes the water to three elements: ozone, hydrogen peroxide, and ultraviolet light. This process destroys the toxic molecules found in some hazardous industrial chemicals. The final product is as clean, or cleaner, than regular tap water or bottled water. According to Wade Miller, executive director of the WateReuse Research Foundation, "By the time the water is through those three processes, it is near distilled quality."[28] Distilled water is boiled and the steam is captured and cooled. The process makes water extremely pure by removing 99.5 percent of minerals and chemical impurities.

WORDS IN CONTEXT

oxidation

the process of being combined chemically with oxygen; a practice that can purify water

A Solar Water Purifier

Most facilities that recycle wastewater into potable freshwater are located in industrialized nations where utilities have the infrastructure to process sewage and treat freshwater. But many parts of the developing world lack efficient municipal water systems. This leaves around 1.1 billion people without clean drinking water. Diseases caused by dirty water kill hundreds of people every day.

In 2012, when New Hampshire student Deepika Kurup was thirteen, she witnessed problems caused by tainted water firsthand when she traveled with her family to India. As Karup later explained, "I saw kids being forced to drink water that is too dirty. So dirty, that I wouldn't even touch it. . . . [This] compelled me to try and address the water crisis." Kurup was passionate about science and understood that two inexpensive chemicals—titanium oxide and zinc oxide—undergo a chemical change when exposed to sunlight. The chemicals produce molecules that attack and destroy certain types of deadly bacteria found in water. Kurup used this knowledge to invent what she called "a Novel Photocatalytic Pervious Composite for Degrading Organics and Inactivating Bacteria in Wastewater." The inexpensive device with the tongue-twisting name purifies drinking water to standards set by the EPA.

Kurup's invention brought her media attention and several awards. In 2012 she won the Discovery Education 3M Young Scientist Challenge along with $25,000. Kurup also won the 2014 Stockholm Junior Water Prize. Her innovation also made her a finalist in the 2015 Google Science Fair and a winner of the National Geographic Explorer Award.

Quoted in Lucas Cocco, "Is Deepika Kurup the Most Talented Freshman at Harvard?," Tab, 2016. http://thetab.com.

The Living Machine ■

Large municipal DPR facilities are not the only way to recycle wastewater. Engineers are now designing on-site wastewater reuse systems that produce nonpotable water for use in large buildings. Rather than rely on a centralized system linked by miles of water mains, the new systems treat wastewater in an individual building or in a number of buildings linked together into a small water recycling district. The systems purify two types of waste: graywater, which is wastewater from bathroom sinks, showers, and washing machines; and blackwater, which comes from toilets, kitchen sinks, and dishwashers. Other sources for on-site wastewater reuse systems include rainwater collected from rooftop surfaces and precipitation that flows into a building's storm drains.

In a typical commercial office building only 5 percent of the water is used for human consumption. The other 95 percent is used for toilet flushing, landscaping irrigation, cooling and heating applications, dust control, fountains and water features, and washing. Nonpotable water, provided by on-site water recycling systems, can be used for these purposes.

One of the most technologically advanced water recycling systems in the world can be found in the headquarters of the San Francisco Public Utilities Commission, the government agency that provides San Francisco with its water. The glimmering thirteen-story building, completed in 2012, was designed to be the greenest urban office building in the United States. The $200 million structure has wind turbines, solar panels, and a wastewater treatment facility known as the Living Machine. The utilities commission website calls the Living Machine "the nation's most cutting-edge onsite water reuse [system]."[29]

Every weekday the Living Machine recycles 5,000 gallons (18,927 L) of graywater and blackwater produced by the commission's nine hundred employees. The raw sewage flows into a 10,000-gallon (37,854 L) tank divided into two compartments. This so-called trash tank filters out fecal matter and other solids, while the settling tank allows finer material to settle to the bottom. This sludge is pumped into the building's sewer pipes, which take it to the municipal wastewater plant.

The next step in the process is one of the most unusual aspects of the Living Machine and is where the system derives its name. A feature called the tidal flow wetlands consists of large planter boxes filled with gravel, located outdoors adjacent to the building. The wetlands contain living organisms such as aquatic plants, algae, snails, and helpful bacteria that work together to decontaminate water. In a process that mimics the water-cleansing effects of natural tidal wetlands, the water is pumped into the boxes from the bottom and then drains back into a recirculation tank. This process occurs twelve times a day.

The next feature in the Living Machine treatment process is called the polishing vertical flow wetlands. Rather than pump the water in from the bottom, the effluent drips down through a gravel bed from the top. The gravel bed filters out the remaining organic material and chemicals like ammonia and dissolved solids. The water is then filtered, exposed to ultraviolet light, and lightly chlorinated. The final product is stored in a recycled-water tank and is used for flushing the building's toilets. The Living Machine reduces total water use in the SFPUC headquarters by 65 percent.

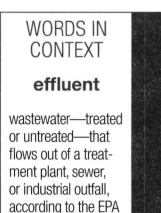

WORDS IN CONTEXT

effluent

wastewater—treated or untreated—that flows out of a treatment plant, sewer, or industrial outfall, according to the EPA

After the success of the Living Machine was demonstrated, San Francisco officials were determined to put similar systems to work in other large buildings. In 2015 San Francisco became the first city in the nation to require on-site water reuse systems in any new developments larger than 250,000 square feet (23,000 m²)—which is about the size of a typical sixteen-story office building. New San Francisco office and residential buildings are now being designed with pipes, tanks, and filtration systems engineered to collect, treat, and recycle graywater and blackwater.

Worms Cleaning Water ■

The Living Machine relies on living organisms to help purify water. This concept is also at the center of a system designed by a Chilean company called BioFiltro. The company's BIDA System is powered by earthworms and bacteria. Earthworms turn organic material such as rotting leaves and manure into a rich, nutrient-laden soil called humus or worm castings. Worms also make numerous channels as they inch their way through the soil. This process aerates, or lets air into, the compacted dirt. Aeration allows beneficial bacteria to grow and break down organic matter in the soil. Earthworms are so important that they were praised by naturalist Charles Darwin in 1881: "Without the work of this humble creature agriculture, as we know it, would be very difficult, if not wholly impossible."[30]

The Living Machine (pictured) is a sophisticated water reuse system that incorporates a simulated ecosystem to decontaminate treated wastewater. The ecosystem consists of living organisms, such as aquatic plants, algae, and snails, that break down pollutants.

Although earthworms have long been well regarded by gardeners and farmers, there was no method to use the creatures in wastewater treatment until Chilean biophysicist José Tohá Castellá invented the BioFiltro technology in the late 1990s. Tohá Castellá understood that 70 percent of the world's supply of freshwater is used in agriculture, and he wanted to find a way to recycle wastewater for farming purposes.

The BioFiltro system consists of large concrete treatment boxes with open chambers at the bottom. The boxes are filled with large river rocks topped by a 3-foot (0.9 m) layer of wood shavings. Each cubic yard (.08 m³) of the wood shavings is home to twelve thousand earthworms and billions of bacteria. Wastewater is sprayed on top of the worm piles, and the creatures thrive in the moist environment. As the water filters down through the wood shavings, the worms eat large pieces of solid matter in the wastewater, while the bacteria eat the microscopic waste. Humus is left behind, while the separated wastewater can be spread on the land, where it filters into the groundwater to be used again in irrigation. BioFiltro's regional manager Mai Ann Healy explains the system:

> Worms target the solids and break this waste down in their stomachs. Their excrement [is] rich in microbial activity. The bacteria are aerobic, needing air to function. The burrowing of earthworms creates air channels throughout, thereby bringing in air and creating an ideal living environment. This [interactive] relationship between worms and bacteria is what powers BioFiltro's systems.[31]

In 2016 there were 140 BIDA Systems cleaning wastewater in six countries. The systems are used at slaughterhouses, dairies, wineries, fish farms, and food production companies. Although the water is not potable, it can be recycled for irrigation and industrial purposes. In 2016 the earthworms and bacteria were put to work at the Fetzer Vineyards in California's Mendocino County. Fetzer has long focused on sustainability. (The winery has been powered by solar panels since 1999.) Vineyards require large quantities of water to grow grapes, produce wine, and clean equipment. The Fetzer facility uses three BIDA treatment boxes, each one 36 feet (11 m) wide, 200 feet (61 m) long, and 6 feet deep (2 m). The boxes hold around 100 million California red worms which digest the solids in the wastewater and produce clean recycled water. The BioFiltro process is faster and cheaper than aeration ponds, which are used to treat wastewater at most wineries. With traditional aeration, wastewater is transferred to settling ponds where large electric pumps constantly mix the water, an energy-intensive process that allows beneficial bacteria to thrive. Whereas the aeration process takes weeks or even months to clean wastewater, the BioFiltro system accomplished the same task in just four days. And its worm castings product is collected from beneath the

WORDS IN CONTEXT

humus

decomposed leaves and other organic material in the soil produced by earthworms, insects, and microorganisms

Purple Pipelines

Direct potable reuse is not the only method to utilize treated wastewater. In some cities nonpotable water that meets EPA standards is recycled for use in irrigation and industry. In California 10 million gallons (37.8 million L) of nonpotable water produced from recycled wastewater is piped into a special system that extends to San Jose, Santa Clara, Milpitas, and other nearby cities. The pipes and hydrants in the 143-mile (230 km) network are purple—a color that designates the network as carrying nonpotable water.

The purple pipeline water is used on grass and plants at local shopping malls, stadiums, government buildings, college campuses, golf courses, parks, and businesses. Some buildings along the network have two plumbing hookups indoors: one line brings in freshwater, and a purple line delivers recycled water. The water in the purple pipes is used for flushing toilets and cooling equipment in air conditioners and power generators. Proponents of the purple pipeline system point out that it is wasteful to use pristine drinking water in toilets. As Gil Friend, the chief sustainability officer for the city of Palo Alto, explains, "Future generations are going to look at us like we're insane that we used drinking water to flush poop. Who could possibly have thought of something so stupid? But here we are."

Quoted in Tara Lohan, "How California Is Learning to Love Drinking Recycled Water," KQED, October 6, 2016. ww2.kqed.org.

boxes several times a year and spread throughout the vineyard to nourish the soil.

Clean Water for a Developing World ■

Although earthworms can be used to clarify water at wineries, dairies, and other small enterprises, Microsoft founder Bill Gates and his wife, Melinda, are funding research to create low-cost facilities that can treat sewage and recycle wastewater in developing nations. The Bill and Melinda Gates Foundation launched its Water, Sanitation, and Hygiene Program in 2010. Since that time the Gates Foundation has challenged engineers and inventors to devise new ways to inexpensively treat sewage and produce

Earthworms turn organic material such as rotting leaves and manure into nutrient-laden worm castings (pictured). A Chilean company has invented a wastewater recycling system that is powered by earthworms and bacteria.

potable water. The need for such facilities is enormous. Around 2.5 billion people—40 percent of the global population—lack toilets or use facilities that do not safely dispose of human waste. In developing nations poor sewage disposal practices kill millions of people every year, many of them children. And half of all patients in hospitals in developing nations are sick because of problems linked to contaminated water and inadequate sanitation. In India alone, poor sanitation costs the nation $54 billion annually in lost work time and increased medical expenses.

In 2015 engineer Peter Janicki built a prototype invention in Sedro-Woolley, Washington, to address these matters. The Janicki Omni Processor simultaneously disposes of sewage, creates potable water, and generates steam-powered electricity. And the processes feed off each other in an energy-efficient loop.

The Janicki Omni Processor is about the size of two school buses, one stacked on top of the other. The process begins when sewage is fed into the machine on a conveyor belt. The waste passes through a series of large heating tubes that boil the sludge. The boiling process separates the water vapor from the solids in the sewage. The dried solids are fed into a furnace that produces high-temperature steam. The steam drives a generator that produces electricity to power the sewage boilers and other processor functions. The processor also produces excess electricity, which feeds into the power grid and is delivered to the local community.

The water vapor created in the boiling process is filtered and condenses back into liquid and runs through a cleaning system. A series of fine mesh and charcoal filters removes any additional substances. The final product is pure, drinkable water that meets or exceeds EPA standards. The furnace in the processor produces nontoxic ash that is high in potassium and phosphorus and can be used as fertilizer.

The Janicki Omni Processor can process 14 tons (12.7 t) of sewage every day— enough to satisfy the potable water and electricity needs of one hundred thousand people. When Bill Gates saw the processor in action in January 2015, he said, "If you can get thousands of these things out there, then you've ensured the people [in developing nations] really will grow up in a healthy way. They'll live much higher quality lives. You will save a lot of lives."[32]

Water Today and Tomorrow ▪

The benefits of recycled water have been appreciated for years by astronauts in the International Space Station (ISS). Since water must be transported to the ISS from Earth, the space station contains an onboard water recovery system. The system recycles 90 percent of the liquid sewage created by the crew, converting it into pure drinking water. Although people might be squeamish about drinking this water, crew commander Koichi Wakata does not have a problem. In a 2015 video demonstrating the ISS water recovery system, Wakata stated, "Here on board the ISS, we turn yesterday's coffee into tomorrow's coffee."[33]

Though some might view the astronaut's statement as a joke, the fact is that the ISS is a microcosm of Earth. Every drop of freshwater on the planet has been recycled through people and animals for countless millennia. There is a finite amount of freshwater available on Earth, and whatever people are drinking today will undoubtedly quench the thirst of someone else tomorrow.

CHAPTER 5

SOLUTIONS:
Transporting Water

"There's plenty of water in the south, not much water in the north. If at all possible, borrowing some water [from the south] would be good."

—Mao Zedong, founder of the People's Republic of China

Quoted in Edward Wong, "Plan for China's Water Crisis Spurs Concern," *New York Times*, June 1, 2011. www.nytimes.com.

Freshwater is not evenly distributed around the world. Some places that desperately need water have none, while others have much more than residents can ever consume. In Australia around 25 percent of all freshwater can be found on the Cape York Peninsula. Parts of this largely unpopulated wilderness area in Far North Queensland receive up to 80 inches (203 cm) of rain a year. But in southern Australia, the capital city of Canberra receives only 20 inches (51 cm) of annual precipitation. And southern cities like Sydney face severe water shortages due to drought and a growing urban population.

The United States is another country with extremely uneven freshwater distribution. The parched Southwest—from Texas to Arizona to California—receives little precipitation and has a very limited groundwater supply. This is not a problem in the rainy and snowy Midwest, where people draw their water from the Great Lakes, the largest freshwater resource on Earth.

Throughout history visionaries have dreamed of transporting water from wet regions to thirsty cities where water is in short supply. During the last century engineers seriously considered seemingly impossible proposals. Some drew up plans to tow icebergs from the Arctic to California. Others dreamed of shipping ice and snow from the Midwest to the sunbaked deserts of the Southwest. During the 1990s a proposal called the Alaskan Subsea Pipeline involved building a 1,400-mile-long (2,253 km) pipeline. The project would have pumped water from Alaskan rivers into a pipe that plunged under the Pacific Ocean in British Columbia, sending water to fill Lake Shasta in Northern California.

Projects like the Alaskan Subsea Pipeline, however unworkable, fall into the category of geoengineering. This branch of science combines elements of transportation, mining, and civil engineering to address problems related to climate and geography. Although many geoengineering schemes have proved impractical, record-breaking droughts in recent years have seen people revitalizing grand plans to move freshwater through pipelines, dams,

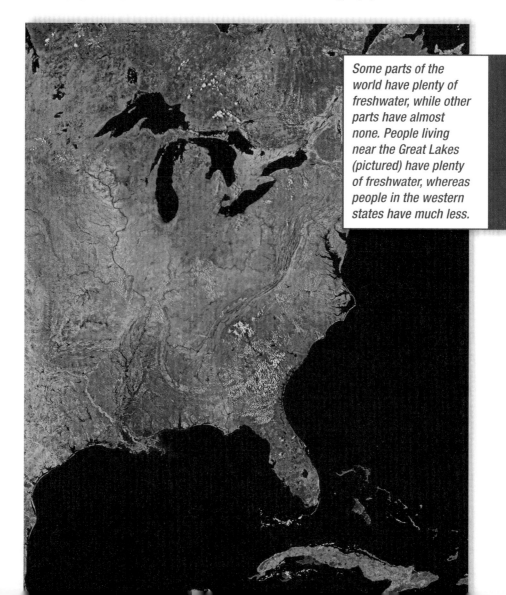

Some parts of the world have plenty of freshwater, while other parts have almost none. People living near the Great Lakes (pictured) have plenty of freshwater, whereas people in the western states have much less.

canals, tunnels, and aqueducts. In 2015 actor William Shatner, who starred in the *Star Trek* television series during the 1960s, proposed building a pipeline from the rainy state of Washington to arid Nevada. Shatner even figured out a way to pay for it, as he told reporter David Pogue: "I'm starting a Kickstarter campaign. I want $30 billion to build a pipeline . . . from Seattle—a place where there's a lot of water. There's too much water. . . . Bring it down here and fill one of our lakes! Lake Mead [in Nevada]!"[34]

Tapping Africa's Water ■

Shatner's proposal has been dismissed as unworkable by water engineers. Such a pipeline would have to be around 1,200 miles (1,931 km) long and cross several mountain chains. Although engineers could theoretically build such a project, it provides an example of why long pipelines pose major engineering challenges. Pipelines are expensive to build and maintain, and moving water requires massive amounts of energy. Pipelines, pumps, and other equipment can leak, corrode, and break, which means the infrastructure requires daily maintenance. Pipelines are also extremely hard on the environment; they can disrupt natural water ecosystems and displace wildlife.

The difficulties surrounding major water pipeline projects are exemplified in a proposal known as the Trans Africa Pipeline (TAP). Conceived by a Canadian nonprofit organization in 2005, the TAP would be a 4,970-mile-long (8,000 km) water pipe. In 2016 the TAP team members were still attempting to raise $20 billion to fund the project. The proposed pipeline would carry freshwater from the West African nation of Mauritania; across the arid regions of eleven countries, including Mali, Niger, and Sudan; and terminate in Djibouti, a nation on the Red Sea.

The area selected for the pipeline is called the Sahel, an arid zone of scrubland that bisects Africa south of the Sahara Desert and north of the African rain forest. The rural region, home to 30 million people, gets 4 to 24 inches (10 to 61 cm) of rain annually but has historically gone through years of long-term drought. In the twenty-first century, a drought that began in 2012 and stretched into 2016 left half the region's population without enough food to eat. The UN says that the Sahel region is one of the places on Earth most prone to droughts caused by climate change.

The pipeline would transport freshwater produced by four high-tech solar-powered desalination plants, two on each coast. Pumping stations, reservoirs, and tank farms would be built about every 125 miles (200 km) along the pipeline route. The TAP website explains important aspects of the pipeline:

> The TAP project will begin to alleviate human dehydration, reduce diseases caused by infected water and poor sanitation, mitigate agricultural drought, and begin the transformation of this region back to a self-sustaining existence. . . . As the population-wide health improves, and the number of family farms increases, cultivation and export of food products will reduce poverty.[35]

The TAP organization also hopes to grow what it calls the Great Green Wall: a 9-mile-wide (14 km) wall of trees and bushes planted along the route, irrigated with water from the pipeline. The Great Green Wall would slow the southward march of the Sahara Desert, which is threatening to turn the Sahel region into a lifeless desert.

Few doubt that the TAP would provide much-needed water to an arid region. But planners believe it will take until 2025—two decades after the project was proposed— to raise the large sum needed for construction. Meanwhile, the political situation in some of the nations along the pipeline route

WORDS IN CONTEXT

tank farm

an area where numerous oil, chemical, or water tanks are located

has deteriorated due to drought conditions destroying economic opportunities. The drought has contributed to political instability in Mali and other nations, giving rise to Islamic terrorist groups. The terrorists often target infrastructure projects such as oil and gas pipelines. There are fears that if the TAP was built, it would become a major target for terrorist bombs.

WaterFix in California ■

One of the safest ways to transport water is through underground aqueducts. However, in terms of infrastructure, nothing is as costly as constructing a tunnel. When engineers want to dig tunnels, they have to draw up tens of thousands of blueprints that include every detail of the project. The main work is performed by giant hole diggers called tunnel boring machines, which are often custom built for each job at great expense. Tunnel construction also requires an army of skilled workers who are moved in and out of the construction zone by elevators and shuttle trains. Construction of walkways, access points, monitoring stations, sanitation facilities, and other infrastructure adds to a tunnel's price. That is why a pair of proposed water tunnels in Northern California would cost $15 billion, or $500 million per mile.

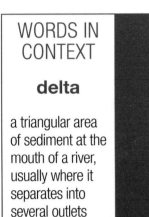

WORDS IN CONTEXT

delta

a triangular area of sediment at the mouth of a river, usually where it separates into several outlets

The tunnel project is formally known as California WaterFix. It would consist of two 30-mile-long (48 km) tunnels running side by side. The tunnels would be 40 feet wide (12 m) and located 150 feet (46 m) below the surface. The WaterFix tunnels would be located below a large expanse of land known as the Delta, where five rivers converge. The main rivers are the Sacramento and the San Joaquin, and the region is often referred to as the Sacramento-San Joaquin Delta.

About half of the total river water in California flows through the 1,100-square-mile (2,849 km²) Sacramento-San Joaquin Delta. Enormous pumps transfer the water into the California Aqueduct and the Delta-Mendota Canal. These concrete channels are the liquid lifelines that deliver water to 20 million people in central and Southern California. The water also provides irrigation to the $36 billion agricultural industry in the Central Valley, which runs through the middle of the state. Journalist Alexis C. Madrigal describes the importance of the Delta:

> It is some of the most important plumbing in the world. Without this crucial nexus point, the current level of agricultural production in the southern San Joaquin Valley could not be sustained, and many cities, including the three largest on the West Coast—Los Angeles, San Diego, and San Jose—would have to come up with radical new water-supply solutions.[36]

Competing water needs in California threaten the state's human and wildlife populations. Delta smelt (pictured) are among the fish that are disappearing from the Sacramento-San Joaquin Delta as water levels have fallen to precipitously low levels.

Delta Threats ■

Although the water allows millions of people to thrive, the aquatic ecosystem of the Delta is collapsing. The once bountiful stocks of Chinook salmon, sturgeon, and other fish species have nearly disappeared due to low water levels and other problems. For example, the Delta smelt population has gone from several million to only about thirty thousand since the 1980s. The tiny fish, which are around 2 inches (5 cm) long, are ground into pulp by the massive water pumps sucking water out of the Delta. At least thirty-five native fish, plant, and animal species living in the Delta are listed under federal and state endangered species acts. Acting under orders from the US Fish and Wildlife Service to protect the smelt and other species, water managers have been forced to cut back on the amount of water pumped from the Delta.

The infrastructure of the Delta is also under threat. In the late 1800s settlers drained the marshes in the area and built a series of levees. These long walls hold back the seawater from the nearby San Francisco Bay that once mingled with the freshwater in the Delta. There are fears that an earthquake or other natural disaster might cause the levees to fail. This would allow saltwater to flow into the Delta, destroying California's major source of freshwater.

The WaterFix is meant to provide engineering solutions to the Delta's environmental problems. The proposed pair of large tunnels, each four stories tall, would pull water from the Sacramento River in the north through three intake stations built near the town of Courtland. Around 67,000 gallons (253,622 L) of water per second would flow through the tunnels under the Delta to the California Aqueduct in the south. Fish screens would keep the aquatic creatures from being pulled into the tunnels. Once the project was completed, the state would spend around $8 billion restoring and protecting around 15,500 acres (6,070 ha) of damaged Delta habitat.

WORDS IN CONTEXT

levee

an embankment of dirt, rocks, or other materials built to prevent the overflow of a river

Building California WaterFix will not be easy. The lives of local residents would be impacted by the huge construction project that would take years to complete. And there are unknown environmental impacts associated with diverting so much freshwater away from the Delta. Additionally, the cost of the project makes it controversial. The engineering feat would create two of the largest tunnels on Earth, rivaling the Chunnel, the tunnel beneath the English Channel connecting France to Great Britain. And for all its expense, WaterFix will not create more water.

China's Giant Pipeline ■

However big California's water problems might be, they are less severe than the water calamity facing the People's Republic of China. After experiencing several decades of growing population, economic expansion, shrinking rainfall, and prolonged drought, thousands of rivers and lakes in China have either dried up and disappeared or have turned into industrial sewers.

China's water distribution is opposite of California's—it is wetter in the south than in the north. However, more than 300 million people—around a quarter of the population—live in northern China, a region that includes the capital city of Beijing. Northern China is home to 42 percent of the nation's population but only

Towing Icebergs

During the last century one of the more popular schemes for transporting freshwater involved moving icebergs from frigid oceans to dry, arid regions. Engineers envisioned towing icebergs with ships or even mounting sails or ship engines directly onto icebergs. In 1973 the concept was taken seriously by the Rand Corporation, a respected think tank. Rand published a report for the National Science Foundation titled *Antarctic Icebergs As a Global Freshwater Resource.* The report noted, "For a thirsty area of the world, the possibility of using Antarctic icebergs as a fresh water resource might become a very attractive prospect."

The authors of the Rand report imagined creating an iceberg train, formed by linking numerous icebergs together in a chain about 12 miles (19 km) long. The iceberg train would be engineered to move through the ocean with an onboard nuclear engine similar to those used in submarines and aircraft carriers. According to Rand, "This operation could potentially satisfy the water demands of an urban population of 500 million, and have a direct economic impact of as much as $10 billion annually."

In 2011 French engineer Georges Mougin created an organization called IceDream to revive the concept of towing icebergs. IceDream determined that a 30-million-ton (27.2 million t) iceberg could supply freshwater to half a million people for one year. The group believed that only 38 percent of the iceberg would melt on its journey if the underside was wrapped in a giant synthetic fabric skirt that would act as insulation.

J.L. Hunt and N.C. Ostrander, "Antarctic Icebergs as a Global Freshwater Resource," Rand Corporation, October 1973. www.rand.org.

contains 8 percent of its water resources. Many of China's factories, ports, and oil production facilities are located in northern China, which makes the region central to the country's economy. However, one of the main water sources in the north, the Yellow River, slows to a trickle almost every summer. In the province of Hebei, which borders Beijing, 969 lakes out of 1,052 have dried up—local farmers now water their fields with sewage.

About 80 percent of China's water can be found in the Yangtze River basin in the southern part of the country. The Chinese government began piping this water north in 2014 when the first segment of the South-to-North Water Diversion Project (SNWDP) opened. This portion of the pipeline supplies freshwater to Beijing, where it is desperately needed.

When all three sections of the SNWDP are completed in 2050, the pipeline will be 2,700 miles (4,350 km) long. This will make it the largest water pipeline—and the most advanced water engineering project—on Earth. The SNWDP will move nearly 12 trillion gallons (45.4 trillion L) of water from the Yangtze River basin to northern regions every year. The project will include the longest canals in the world, underground pipelines that cross wide riverbeds, and immense pumping stations that move hundreds of thousands of gallons of water every minute.

Doubts About the Pipeline ■

Nothing like the SNWDP exists anywhere in the world. If it were to be built in the United States, it would nearly stretch from coast to coast. The SNWDP will pass through fifteen of the nation's twenty-two provinces and cost more than $60 billion. Construction will destroy hundreds of ancient archaeological and religious sites that lie in the pipeline path and force half a million people to relocate.

Even with all the disruption, there are doubts that the pipeline will solve China's water problems. The government is taking water away from people in wetter southern regions that depend on the rivers for survival. For example, the Yangtze is the main water supply for 400 million people, and water levels have been dropping due to climate change. The Yangtze is fed by snowmelt in the Himalayas. Since the early 2010s, the mountains have received less snow. The amount of freshwater flowing into the Yangtze has plunged by nearly 20 percent. In addition, when the waters are diverted north by the pipeline, the lowered water levels will destroy wetlands that harbor a wide variety of birds, fish, and other creatures.

The decreased water volume is adding to pollution problems by weakening the river's ability to cleanse itself. Some parts of the Yangtze have been called cancerous, and this water will be sent thousands of miles through pipelines to northern China. In order to reduce pollution, officials are forcing factories along the river to shut down, putting thousands out of work.

This tunnel runs under the Yellow River and forms part of China's South-to-North Water Diversion Project. The project is part of a multibillion-dollar effort to bring water from the Yangtze River to the country's thirsty northern regions.

Engineers Moving Water ■

Although the SNWDP now delivers water to Beijing from the south, the city continues to face shortages. The pipeline supplies 317 billion gallons (1.2 trillion L) of water annually, but Beijing's current shortfall is 396 billion gallons (1.5 trillion L). And the population is expected to explode in China's capital in the coming years, which will only aggravate Beijing's water shortages. As with California WaterFix, the SNWDP will not create more water—it will just move it around at great fiscal and environmental expense. Despite the SNWDP's many shortcomings, Chinese leaders felt that something needed to be done to bring water to the arid north. It was then up to the engineers to draw up plans for grand projects designed to reshape China's rivers on a scale unprecedented in human history.

Wherever they live, engineers have long played a role in moving water from one place to another. The pipes, tunnels, aqueducts,

Beijing's Water Problems

China's massive South-to-North Water Diversion Project (SNWDP) is an engineering miracle that began providing desperately needed water to Beijing in 2014. China's capital is the third most populous city in the world with a metropolitan population of nearly 25 million. Although the city was once known for its abundant streams and freshwater springs, modern Beijing is one of the most water-scarce cities on Earth. Every day Beijing residents consume about 75 percent more water than is available from local rivers and aquifers. The city diverts water from the nearby Hebei province, which has seen hundreds of its lakes drained.

Beijing was always arid, but average annual rainfall has declined substantially in recent decades due to climate change. The rivers that appear on city maps are empty riverbeds most of the year. Pollution adds to the city's problems. Beijing residents traditionally took their water from the Yongding River, but this source was abandoned in 1997 when the river water became too polluted with industrial wastewater. Today Beijing receives 75 percent of its water from an aquifer below the city. But groundwater levels are falling 3 feet (1 m) a year. No one knows how deep the aquifer is, but that rate of outflow is not sustainable. Officials try to encourage residents to conserve water, but with its exploding population, Beijing's water problems will not be easily solved.

reservoirs, and pumping stations make up some of the most complex infrastructure on Earth. And every detail originated with drawings, calculations, and models made by engineers. Although rain, rivers, lakes, and aquifers are the products of nature, the paths that transport that water to billions of people are part of the work performed every day by engineers.

SOURCE NOTES

INTRODUCTION
Clean Water in a Dirty World

1. Robert Kandel, *Water from Heaven.* New York: Columbia University Press, 2003, p. 2.
2. Steven Solomon, *Water: The Epic Struggle for Wealth, Power, and Civilization.* New York: HarperCollins, 2010, p. 21.

CHAPTER 1
CURRENT STATUS: How Clean Water Is Provided

3. Quoted in Melanie Burford and Greg Moyer, "A Marvel of Engineering Meets the Needs of a Thirsty New York," *New York Times*, October 16, 2014. www.nytimes.com.
4. Alfred Douglas Finn, "The World's Greatest Aqueduct," Catskill Archive, 2010. http://catskillarchive.com.
5. Quoted in Cristian Salazar, "How New York City Gets Its Water: From Reservoir to Tap," AM New York, April 30, 2016. www.amny.com.
6. Quoted in James Salzman, "A Toast to the Safe Drinking Water Act," *Slate,* December 14, 2014. www.slate.com.
7. Quoted in Sharon Benzoni, "Tiny Bags of Water Buoy an Economy, and Make a Big Mess," Informal City Dialogs, August 12, 2013. https://nextcity.org.
8. Benzoni, "Tiny Bags of Water Buoy an Economy, and Make a Big Mess."
9. James Salzman, "A Toast to the Safe Drinking Water Act," *Slate,* December 14, 2014. www.slate.com.

CHAPTER 2
PROBLEMS: Pollution, Waste, and Drought

10. Quoted in Merrit Kennedy, "Lead-Laced Water in Flint: A Step-by-Step Look at the Makings of a Crisis," NPR, April 20, 2016. www.npr.org.

11. Quoted in Alejandro Dávila Fragoso, "Flint Groups File Suit Asking for Lead Free Pipes as Polluted Water Corrodes the System," Think Progress, January 27, 2016. https://think progress.org.
12. Quoted in Adam Wernick, "An Investigation Has Found Lead in 2,000 Water Systems," PRI, April 9, 2016. www .pri.org.
13. Quoted in Raw Story, "This Quote from Rick Snyder's Emails Says Everything You Need to Know About Flint's Water Crisis," January 29, 2016. www.rawstory.com.
14. Office of the Press Secretary, "Fact Sheet: Working Together to Build a Sustainable Water Future," White House, March 22, 2016. www.whitehouse.gov.
15. Quoted in Rosanna Xia, "Many of the World's Water Basins Are Being Depleted, Study Finds," *Los Angeles Times,* June 17, 2015. www.latimes.com.

CHAPTER 3
SOLUTIONS: Transforming Seawater to Freshwater

16. Quoted in James Stafford, "The Game-Changing Water Revolution: Interview with Stanley Weiner," OilPrice.com, April 13, 2015. http://oilprice.com.
17. Solomon, *Water,* p. 21.
18. Quoted in Matt Weiser, "Could Desalination Solve California's Water Problem?," *Sacramento Bee*, October 14, 2015. www .sacbee.com.
19. Brian Bienkowski, "Desalination Is an Expensive Energy Hog, but Improvements Are on the Way," PRI, May 15, 2015. www .pri.org.
20. Quoted in Elsevier, "Can Engineered Carbon Nanotubes Help to Avert Our Water Crisis?," March 17, 2015. www.elsevier .com.
21. Quoted in Kent Harrington, "Saudi Arabia Creates New Solar-Powered Desalination Technology," ChEnected, October 16, 2015. www.aiche.org.

22. Quoted in Science Daily, "New Desalination Technology Could Answer State Drought Woes," February 17, 2015. www.sciencedaily.com.
23. *Yale Scientific,* "Engineering Clean Water," April 3, 2011. www.yalescientific.org.

CHAPTER 4
SOLUTIONS: Recycling Wastewater

24. Matt Weiser, "Wastewater: A New Frontier for Water Recycling," Water Deeply, September 20, 2016. www.newsdeeply.com.
25. Quoted in Monte Morin, "Turning Sewage into Drinking Water Gains Appeal as Drought Lingers," *Los Angeles Times*, May 24, 2015. www.latimes.com.
26. Quoted in Rashda Khan, "A Tale of Three Texas Cities and Water Reuse," *San Angelo Standard-Times,* April 9, 2016. http://archive.gosanangelo.com.
27. Quoted in Khan, "A Tale of Three Texas Cities and Water Reuse."
28. Quoted in Sarah Fister Gale, "Battling Water Scarcity: Direct Potable Reuse Poised as Future of Water Recycling," *WaterWorld*, 2016. www.waterworld.com.
29. San Francisco Public Utilities Commission, "Living Machine at 525 Golden Gate Ave," 2015. http://sfwater.org.
30. Quoted in BioFiltro, "Catalyze Natural Processes," 2016. http://biofiltro.com.
31. Quoted in Peak Johnson, "Earthworms Star in Latest Wastewater Filtration Tech," Water Online, May 13, 2016. www.wateronline.com.
32. Quoted in Davey Alba, "Bill Gates' Plan to Help the Developing World Profit from Its Sewage," *Wired,* January 6, 2015. www.wired.com.
33. Quoted in Elizabeth Howell, "'Yesterday's Coffee': Drinking Urine in Space Could Preview Mars Exploration Techniques," Universe Today, December 23, 2015. www.universetoday.com.

CHAPTER 5
SOLUTIONS: Transporting Water

34. Quoted in David Pogue, "Exclusive: William Shatner's $30 Billion Kickstarter Campaign to Save California," Yahoo! News, April 17, 2015. www.yahoo.com.

35. Trans Africa Pipeline, "About Us: The TAP Journey," 2016. http://transafricapipeline.org.

36. Alexis C. Madrigal, "American Aqueduct: The Great California Water Saga," *Atlantic*, February 24, 2014. www.theatlantic .com.

Books

Bridget Heos, *It's Getting Hot in Here: The Past, Present, and Future of Climate.* Boston: HMH Books for Young Readers, 2016.

Stuart A. Kallen, *Running Dry.* Minneapolis: Twenty-First Century, 2015.

Andrea C. Nakaya, *What Are the Consequences of Climate Change?* San Diego: ReferencePoint, 2016.

Bill Nye, *Unstoppable: Harnessing Science to Change the World.* New York: St. Martin's Griffin, 2016.

David Sedlak, *Water 4.0.* New Haven, CT: Yale University Press, 2014.

Websites

Circle of Blue (www.circleofblue.org). In 2000, journalists and scientists founded this website to provide information about the world water crisis and its relationship to food, energy, and health.

Environmental Working Group (www.ewg.org). This organization focuses on environmental research concerning toxic chemicals and human health, farming practices and agricultural chemicals, and the sustainable use of water and other natural resources. Its website encourages student and consumer participation in environmental actions.

Natural Resources Defense Council (www.nrdc.org). Hosted by one of the world's leading environmental organizations, this site provides science-based information about threats to the air, freshwater, and oceans, along with details concerning global warming, factory farming, fracking, and other ecological issues.

Trans Africa Pipeline (http://transafricapipeline.org). Hosted by a Canadian nonprofit organization working to build a massive pipeline across Africa, this website describes the water shortages, the desalination plants, and other topics associated with the project that plans to bring freshwater to 30 million Africans.

Water.org (www.water.org). Cofounded by actor Matt Damon, Water.org focuses on water and sanitation problems in poor countries. Its website provides statistics, maps, photos, and videos that highlight the problems and also offers solutions.

Internet Sources

Sharon Benzoni, "Tiny Bags of Water Buoy an Economy, and Make a Big Mess," Informal City Dialogs, August 12, 2013. https://nextcity.org/informalcity/entry/tiny-bags-of-water-buoy-an-economy-and-make-a-big-mess.

Melanie Burford and Greg Moyer, "A Marvel of Engineering Meets the Needs of a Thirsty New York," *New York Times*, October 16, 2014. www.nytimes.com/2014/10/17/nyregion/new-york-city-water-supply.html?_r=0.

Lily Kug, "China Has Launched the Largest Water-Pipeline Project in History," *Atlantic,* March 7, 2014. www.theatlantic.com/international/archive/2014/03/china-has-launched-the-largest-water-pipeline-project-in-history/284300.

Alexis C. Madrigal, "American Aqueduct: The Great California Water Saga," *Atlantic,* February 24, 2014. www.theatlantic.com/technology/archive/2014/02/american-aqueduct-the-great-california-water-saga/284009.

INDEX

tunnels, 59–62
turbine, defined, 42

United States
  average daily use, 12
  cost of tap versus bottled
    water, 12–13
  drinking water safety, 12
  droughts, 45, 56
  lead in water pipes, 23–24,
    26, 27
  number of municipal water
    supply systems, 12
  toxins in drinking water, 12,
    21
  See also lead
  water distribution
    needs, 56
    pipelines, 23–24, 26, 27,
      53, 57–58
    underground aqueducts,
      59–62
  See also Flint, Michigan;
    specific states
University of California–Los
  Angeles, 34
University of Southern
  California, 41–42
unsustainable, defined, 31

Voltic, 18

Wakata, Koichi, 55
Walling, Dayne, 25
Walters, LeeAnne, 25–26
wastewater recycling
  direct potable reuse
    first US plant, 45
    nickname, 9

  process described, **46**, 47
  yuck factor, 44
  on International Space
    Station, 55
  Janicki Omni Processor,
    54–55
  purple pipelines, 53
  on-site, 48–53, **51**
  solar purifiers, 48
water distribution
  Australia, 56
  China
    needs in, 56, 62–63
    South-to-North Water
      Diversion Project, 64–65,
      65, 66
  Trans Africa Pipeline, 58–59
  United States
    needs, 56
    pipelines, 23–24, 26, 27,
      53, 57–58
    underground aqueducts,
      59–62
  using recycled, 53
  See also pipelines
WaterFX, 43
Weiner, Stanley, 32, 33
Weiser, Matt, 44
West African Republic of
  Ghana, 17, 18–20, **19**
Whitney, Victoria, 38
World Health Organization,
  22
World Water Council, 29
World Water Day, 26

Yale Scientific, 42–43
Yangtze River, 63, 64
Young, Alison, 21, 25

PICTURE CREDITS

Cover: Shutterstock.com/Riccardo Mayer

4: iStockphoto/typhoon ski (top)

4: iStockphoto/Flightlevel80 (middle)

4: Depositphotos/Andrey Popov (bottom)

5: Depositphotos/3DSculptor (top)

5: Depositphotos/-Baks- (middle left)

5: Depositphotos/Cliparea (middle right)

5: iStockphoto/Johavel (bottom)

8: NASA

11: Depositphotos/Rabbit75_dep

14: Depositphotos/iofoto

19: Shutterstock/Anton Ivanov

23: Ryan Garza/Zuma Press/Newscom

27: Shutterstock/photopixel

30: Shutterstock/David Litman

34: Depositphotos/izanbar

36: Maury Aaseng

41: Fahad Shadeed/Reuters/Newscom

46: Maury Aaseng

51: Martin Bond/Science Photo Library

54: Thinkstock Images/iStock

57: Worldsat International, Inc./Science Photo Library

61: Associated Press

65: Associated Press

ABOUT THE AUTHOR

Stuart A. Kallen is the author of more than 350 nonfiction books for children and young adults. He has written on topics ranging from the theory of relativity to the art of electronic dance music. In addition, Kallen has written award-winning children's videos and television scripts. In his spare time he is a singer, songwriter, and guitarist in San Diego.

Abington Public Library
Abington, MA 02351